THE
BIOLOGICAL BASIS
OF
HUMAN FREEDOM

G.

THEODOSIUS DOBZHANSKY

THE
BIOLOGICAL BASIS
OF
HUMAN FREEDOM

New York and London
COLUMBIA UNIVERSITY PRESS

5480

56-11981

Preface

This book is an attempt to interpret some of the philosophical implications of modern biology in terms which a layman can understand. Really fundamental ideas of science should be made comprehensible to people having no special competence in a given branch of science. Once grasped, a great truth becomes self-evident. Unfortunately, the ability to state scientific ideas simply and accurately varies from person to person, and on this score the present writer feels very serious misgivings. Yet, the current surge of anti-intellectualism should stimulate scientists to try to explain to their fellow citizens that science leads not only to the invention of new gadgets and of atomic and other bombs but also to the acquisition of new insights into human nature and man's place in the universe.

The five chapters which compose this book are somewhat expanded versions of the Page-Barbour lectures delivered at the University of Virginia, at Charlottesville, in March of 1954. Of necessity, the argument which is contained in each chapter is presented briefly and with a minimum of supporting references and illustrative examples. To have these arguments adequately hedged with proper reservations would hardly add much to their usefulness to a nonbiologist; a biologist will be able to supply the reservations himself.

The author wishes to express his profound appreciation to the committee on the Page-Barbour lectures for having been the first biologist chosen to deliver these lectures, and to Professor and Mrs. Laddley Husted for their very kind hospitality while at Charlottesville. Several colleagues, particularly Professors Charles L. Birch, L. C. Dunn, and J. A. Moore have contributed greatly to clarification of some of the ideas by discussions and by critical reading of the manuscript.

Contents

Preface   v

Man's Kinship with Nature   3

Heredity as a Basis of Culture   26

Who Is the Fittest?   55

Human and Animal Societies   86

Necessity and Freedom   109

Bibliography   137

THE
BIOLOGICAL BASIS
OF
HUMAN FREEDOM

Man's Kinship with Nature

Man is a rope stretched between the animal and the Superman—a rope over an abyss. Thus spake Zarathustra. FRIEDRICH NIETZSCHE

Creation by Evolution

Informed about Darwin's theory of the origin of man, the wife of the Canon of Worcester Cathedral cried out: "Descended from the apes! My dear, we hope it is not true. But if it is, let us pray that it may not become generally known." The lady felt it very degrading to be related, however distantly, to an ape. The same sentiment has frequently been expressed in a more serious vein. Chaadaev, one of the keenest minds of his time, and one of the most original among Russian philosophers, wrote the following in 1829, more than forty years before the publication of Darwin's *The Descent of Man:* "When philosophy occupies itself with the animal man it ceases to be a philosophy of man and becomes a philosophy of animals, a chapter of zoology dealing with man." Even at present some people still regard evolution as subversive to religion and to morals. Yet most people see in the theory of evolution a reaffirmation of man's dignity and liberation from spiritual bondage.

Evolution is at present more than a biological theory. Evolutionism has influenced the physical as well as the social sciences, and has become an integral part of the intellectual equipment of modern mankind. It should not be forgotten, however, that evolutionary ideas are relatively novel; recognition of the importance of development, of change in nature is a recent phenomenon. Oriental thought preferred to believe in eternal recurrence, rather than in history being directional and on the whole progressive. Myths of the classical world recognized change, but made it regressive rather than progressive. The universe began with a distant Age of Gold, then degenerated to an Age of Iron. Plato, perhaps the greatest thinker of antiquity, regarded the world we live in as merely a distorted reflection of eternal and immutable Ideas, stored forever in some philosophical heaven.

Among the great religions, Christianity is the one which is at least implicitly evolutionistic. To be sure, it accepts the Fall at the beginning of history. But man has fallen only to begin to rise again, and this rise is progressive. Evolution is a cosmic process, the central event of which is the act of Redemption by the Son of God. The climax of the evolutionary development will be the attainment of the City of God. Medieval Christianity found it nevertheless possible to think of Creation not as a gradual process but as an act consummated within the space of six days some fifty-three centuries before. According to this view, the world as we see it today is like an extinct volcano, in which the ancient fires of Creation have died down to the cold ashes of a fixed hierarchy of physical, biological, and spiritual species. The world-machine was perfectly planned, made, and duly set in motion. All that has happened since then was predestined to happen from the beginning. No wonder that many people concluded that the Maker stood aside once the machine was completed, unwilling to interfere in the running of so perfect a mechanism. There is a tremendous gap between this view and the burning words of St. Paul: "Because the creature itself also shall be delivered from the bondage of corruption into the glorious liberty of the children of God. For we know that the whole creation groaneth and travaileth in pain together until now" (Rom. 8: 21–22). The Creation is not complete. It is not an event which happened in the remote past but rather a living reality of the present. Creation is a process of evolution of which man is not merely a witness but a participant and a partner as well.

Evolution: Fact or Hypothesis?

It is not the purpose of this book to present the evidence that evolution in general, and the evolution of man in particular, has actually taken place. This has been done many times by many competent and able authors. Ours is a more limited but less conventional task. It is to show that human evolution is, in major respects, singular and unique in the living world.

Evolutionists since Darwin have concentrated their efforts on proving that man is indeed a biological species, and, as such, is a product of organic evolution. This concentration was a natural, and perhaps a necessary, response to the antievolutionists who stubbornly challenged the validity of what, at least to competent biologists, became almost a commonplace. But the focusing of attention on the commonplace has obscured the biological singularity of man. Man is a most extraordinary product of evolution; he is so much unlike any other biological species that his evolution cannot be adequately understood in terms of only those causative factors which are operating in the biological world outside the human kind. The singularity of human evolution lies in the fact that the human species has evolved culture. Culture is the exclusive property of man. Once man became, to use the pithy words of Aristotle, "a political animal," his biological evolution was profoundly modified; he cannot any longer be understood except as a uniquely human phenomenon.

Evolution as a historical fact was proved beyond reasonable doubt not later than in the closing decades of the nineteenth century. No one who takes the trouble to become familiar with the pertinent evidence has at present a valid reason to disbelieve that the living world, including man, is a product of an evolutionary development. According to the classical saying, "Fata volentem ducunt, nolentem trahunt"—which can be freely translated to mean that "Necessity guides those who accept it, and drags those who resist it." To be sure, antievolutionists still exist. But it is fair to say that most of them are not well informed, while the informed exceptions display biases which make arguments futile and facts useless. Does it indeed make sense to declare oneself unconvinced by the evidence for evolution only because no one has actually seen the "fact" of the transformation of the dawn horse into a present-day horse, or of the prehuman into a human being? This is like the Midwestern gentleman who was unconvinced that the earth was round, even after he took a "round-the-world" trip. Nobody has seen atoms and molecules either, but we act as though atoms and molecules were facts and not hypotheses. Evolution took place mostly before there were observers to see it and to record their observations. Any such historical fact must be inferred on the basis of evidence which can be seen today. It is no mere matter of taste whether one rejects or accepts the inference. A hypothesis may, at a certain level of scientific knowledge, be forced upon every reasonable person.

Innumerable facts of comparative morphology, physiology, embryology, paleontology, and geographic distribution suggest that evolution has taken place. These facts make sense if the hypothesis of evolution is granted; they do not make sense otherwise. Not only new varieties but undoubtedly new species have been created in genetic experiments. But, say the antievolutionists, all this merely suggests, it does not prove, evolution. Even if not in species, then perhaps in genera, or in families, or in classes God may have chosen to install within created entities homologous organs and developmental systems. He may also have chosen to place in the various geological strata such fossils as would be expected to occur if evolution had happened although in reality it did not happen. Whether those who make such arguments realize it or not, these arguments are undoubtedly blasphemous. Can anyone really believe that God would so capriciously and frivolously falsify evidence and lead astray sincere students of His works? It would, indeed, be a monstrous deception, unworthy of the Creator.

This certainly does not mean that we know everything about evolution in general or even about human evolution in particular. Organic evolution, like human history, is a process which was enacted in the past and which is taking place in the present. A process of this sort may be studied in two different, though by no means mutually exclusive, ways. A human historian, as well as a biological historian, may describe and analyze the process in terms of the way it has actually come to pass. In this aspect history is unique—it takes place once and does not repeat itself. But one may also study the processes which occur in nature or in society at our own time level, or which can be made to happen in laboratory experiments or in field observations. Such processes are recurrent, and, at least in principle, can be made to occur at any time. Among them are found the causes of evolutionary changes—of evolutionary history as it actually happened in the past, as well as of all possible evolutions, including those which will actually take place in the future.

There is no doubt that both the historical and the causal aspects of the evolutionary process are far from completely known. Despite numerous discoveries of sub-human and prehuman remains in recent years, no one is audacious enough to reconstruct all the stages through which the development of the human species had passed before the appearance of Homo sapiens, let alone a complete phylogeny of hominoids. The causes which have brought about the development of the human species can be only dimly discerned, and those which resulted in the differentiation of this species into races are obscure. All that this means is that biology in general, and the biology of man in particular, are youthful sciences still at the beginning of their careers. But, while it is dangerous to forget the extent of our ignorance, it is foolish to neglect what we know. For this is incontrovertible: the organisms now existing have descended from very different beings which lived in the past, and man is a biological species which has evolved from ancestors who were not men. Evolution is a historical continuity, a minute part of which can be observed and experimented with during human lifetime, but most of which took place in the past. Past evolution can be studied with methods analogous to those used to study human history, or rather prehistory. But, unlike human history, some events of organic evolution can also be deduced from observations on the processes now going on in living populations.

Biological Forces in Human Evolution

Man is the only biological species which has a highly developed capacity for symbolic thought and for the use of language, and which has built a complex body of tradition known as culture. Culture is an exclusive property of man, and the transmission of culture from generation to generation occurs by means of instruction, precept, imitation, and learning. This is basically different from the transmission of biological heredity, which takes place by means of genes in the sex cells.

The evolutionary pattern of the human species is, accordingly, unique in the living world. To get even a very rough approximation of an understanding of this unique evolutionary pattern, we must inquire into the biological meaning of specifically human attributes, and consider them in the light of what is known about the causative factors of the evolution of life in general. The biological evolution of man has been brought about by the operation of the same basic evolutionary mechanisms which exist in other organisms. To put it in another way, the singularity of human evolution is the outcome of a particular pattern of evolutionary forces rather than the addition of any unfamiliar or inscrutable agent. The influence of culture on the evolutionary pattern of mankind occurs, then, by way of biological causation.

Evolution is change in the heredity, in the genetic endowment, of succeeding generations. Heredity is a conservative force; it tends to make the offspring like their parents and to make future generations like their ancestors. If heredity were perfect there would be no evolution. It is a remarkable combination of stability and changeability which makes heredity the vehicle of evolution. Heredity is the basis of the biological evolution of all forms of life—from viruses and bacteria to mice and men. No biological phenomenon is as universal as heredity;

in fact, heredity is the self-reproduction of the organism using materials taken from the environment, and self-reproduction is life. No understanding of evolution is possible except with the foundation of a knowledge of heredity.

The Nature of Heredity

Probably no other biological concept is so often, so widely, and so persistently misunderstood as that of heredity. The root of the trouble is that everyday language confuses biological heredity with the inheritance of property. This confusion exists not only in English but also in other, at least in European, languages. Now, the inheritance of property means that certain material objects change owners without necessarily undergoing any change themselves in the process. If one inherits a house or a bank account, there exist certain spatio-temporal objects which become the property of the inheritor, but do not become parts of his body. Inheritance of skin color, musical abilities, or criminal tendencies obviously cannot mean the same thing as the inheritance of property. We do not receive from our parents skin or eyes or brain; the only physical connection between the bodies of our parents and we the offspring are the sex cells. The sex cells from which an individual develops must and do contain the sum total of his heredity. But sex cells have no skin, no eyes, no brain, and assuredly no musical abilities.

The school of preformists, which was fashionable in biology especially during the eighteenth century, contended that the male sex cells, spermatozoa, or the female sex cells, the eggs, had in them a miniature model of the organism which would develop from them eventually. Human sex cells were supposed to contain a "homunculus," a tiny but otherwise perfect creature who had only to grow to become an adult. This was, however, a delusion, for sex cells actually have nothing resembling the parts of the body of an adult organism. What sex cells do transmit is a dynamic physiological pattern, a pattern of metabolism, which makes them develop, through a succession of definite stages, into a fertilized egg, a fetus, an infant, a child, a youth, an adult, an old man or an old woman, and, sooner or later, a dead body. The sex cells are, then, merely the vehicles or containers by which we inherit the metabolic patterns which condition the development of our bodies at all stages of life. At certain stages of the developmental process, there appear a certain coloration of the skin, musical or other abilities or their lack, and some temperamental characteristics which, under certain circumstances, may lead a person to become a criminal, a religious leader, a politician, or—a biologist. An individual inherits a developmental pattern for his body as a whole—his body must have a skin, which then develops a certain color; it must have a brain to appreciate music before musical ability can be manifested. Abilities and disabilities are not inherited as separate entities; they are merely aspects of the developmental pattern of the organism.

An estimate, first made by H. J. Muller, shows how

incredibly small are the material carriers of heredity. A human egg cell has a diameter about 0.1 of a mm., and a weight of about 0.0015 mg. (0.000,000,05 of an ounce). All the egg cells which gave rise to the present population of the earth, about two and a half billion of them, would, then, fit easily into a gallon pitcher. An equal number of spermatozoa would have a much smaller volume, less than that of a regular aspirin tablet, according to Muller. The entire bulk of the sex cells—eggs and spermatozoa—is not made up only of genes, the carriers of heredity. For example, the genes in the egg cell have only about the same mass as they do in the much smaller spermatozoon. The aggregate volume of all the genes in all the sex cells which produced the world's population today would probably not exceed that of a vitamin capsule. This tiny mass contains, then, all the biological heredity of the living representatives of our species, and the material basis of its future evolution.

The operation of heredity in bringing about the development of a living individual occurs by means of assimilation of food and of growth. A fertilized human egg cell, the dimensions of which were given above, becomes eventually an adult person who weighs, say, 160 pounds. This is approximately a fifty billion-fold increase in weight. The tremendous increase in mass occurs evidently at the expense of the food which the individual consumes and assimilates, assimilation being a process whereby the food materials derived from the environment are chemically transformed to become the constituents of the living body.

Heredity furnishes the pattern of these transformations, which build a likeness of the assimilating body out of the materials taken in from the environment.

The Gene Theory

Just how the heredity transmitted in the sex cells brings about the development of the organism at different stages of life is far from completely known at present. Some biologists even see fit to suppose that this development is presided over by some mysterious psychic energies. However, the majority of biologists consider it far more probable that the development is ultimately a system of metabolic, and hence physicochemical, reactions. But so enormous is the complexity of this system, even in the simplest organisms such as viruses, that biology and biochemistry are still very far from unraveling the workings of the metabolic machinery of the body.

A discovery made by Gregor Mendel in 1866, forgotten until 1900, and amply confirmed and extended since then, has however revealed some very basic facts about heredity. Heredity is particulate; it is carried in the sex cells in the form of a finite number of corpuscles called genes. A gene is a particle of molecular dimensions, possibly a single complex molecule or a part of a molecular aggregate, a kind of a supermolecule. A sex cell of any species of organism carries a definite set of genes, which preserve their identities during the whole life cycle, and which become segregated and recombined during the formation of the sex cells of the succeeding generation. We can observe the working of the genes especially in the offspring of crosses between parents which differ in some easily visible traits or characteristics of the body. Thus, there are simple rules which permit prediction of the probable distribution of the blood groups among children in families in which parents or grandparents had blood of different types. Similar rules apply to the distribution of eye color among children in certain families, and to the inheritance of many other bodily traits, both normal and pathological. Some gene differences evidently influence blood types, others, eye color, or the ability or inability to taste certain chemical substances, or the normal or abnormal development of certain organs, or physiological functions.

At this point it is necessary to be on one's guard against another possible confusion of biological heredity with inheritance of property. Our heredity is particulate, for we have inherited from our parents a certain number of genes transmitted in the sex cells. But the development of the organism is unitary, because it is conditioned by all the genes which the organism has. In other words, development does not consist of "unit characters" being added one to the other until the organism is complete; it is not that the blood group arises first, then the skin, then the skin color, and then the taste reactions. Rather, what happens is that development as a whole, as well as its various stages, are governed by the whole complex of genes, by the genotype. Development at any given moment is a consequence of preceding developmental stages or events and of the conditions acting on the organism at that particular moment.

Biological shorthand expressions, such as "the gene for eye color," should, then, not be taken too literally. There is no gene which could by itself manufacture an eye, or an eye color, or a taste reaction, or criminal or law-abiding behavior. We do not inherit pigments, or tastes, or behaviors. What we do inherit is a constellation of genes, a genotype. Some human genotypes so condition development that one person has brown eyes, while other genotypes cause the eyes to be blue. To be sure, this difference between developmental patterns may be due to a single gene, and the variant forms of this gene may be called "the gene for brown eyes" or "the gene for blue eyes."

The gene in the sex cell is a mere molecule, far too small to be seen even in the strongest of microscopes. It is a most remarkable phenomenon of nature that in the process of development the effects of this apparently insignificant bit of matter virtually snowballs, and may be magnified so greatly as to become strikingly visible. It is the snowballing of "the gene for eye color" that makes some eyes brown and others blue. A gene-molecule in the sex cell may make the difference between normal health and disease, or between normal intelligence and idiocy. Thus the gene structure contains most efficiently coded information, making the developmental machinery of a body as complex as that of a man operate in one of the many possible ways.

How do the genes influence development? We do not know yet for sure, although some interesting and ingenious speculations have been advanced. Here it may be worth pointing out one kind of function all genes must perform, namely that all of them must be able to reproduce themselves. When a cell divides, the daughter cells each have a copy of all the genes that the mother cell had. These genes must have built their own copies from nongenic materials in the cells. In the last analysis, heredity may be conceived as the sum of processes whereby the gene-molecules make their own copies. Before all else, genes must make more of themselves. They may also serve as sites of important physiological activity in the cells. The specificity of certain cellular enzymes may well be gene-controlled. In a sense, the development of the organism is a by-product of the processes of self-reproduction of the genes. The action of the genes channels the physiological processes in the developing body in such a manner that development follows a certain course, producing a body belonging to a certain species, having eyes of a certain structure, with a certain amount of a coloring matter deposited in the iris. The eye-pigment, and even the eye itself, are not pre-formed in the genes. They arise as a result of a process of development which is a corollary of the self-reproduction of the genes.

Stability of the Genes and Mutation

Rash statements by some biologists have led to a widespread misapprehension that biology considers the genes to be isolated from the environment and unchangeable by external agencies. Nothing can be farther from the truth. Since genes reproduce themselves, they are of necessity in constant interaction with the environment, transforming the susceptible part of the latter (food, in the broadest sense) into their own copies. Far from being inert, genes are perhaps, physiologically and chemically, the most active cell constituents. Most genes are borne in chromosomes which are known to consist of nucleoproteins, nucleoproteins being chemical compounds which can easily be altered by a variety of physical and chemical influences.

The real problem is not whether the genes can be altered by environmental agencies or not, for they obviously can be so altered. The problem is: What are the results of the gene alterations? The evidence bearing on this point is unambiguous in one respect: It shows that most alterations induced into the genes by outside agents make these genes no longer able to reproduce themselves. To put it another way, the genes either continue to produce their own faithful copies of themselves, or, with very rare exceptions, they produce nothing at all. A gene which is not capable of self-reproduction is, however, no longer a gene, that is, in the sense that it is no longer a unit of heredity. There are good reasons to suppose that, in some body cells which no longer divide, the genes continue to function as important agents in the cellular metabolism without reproducing themselves. But genes which have permanently lost this ability of self-reproduction in cells which do divide will, of course, not be present in the progeny of the cell which contained them. Therefore, from a biological standpoint, such genes do not exist.

Only a small minority of the changes which can possibly occur in genes permit the altered genes to reproduce or synthesize copies of the altered structure from non-genic materials. These, and only these, exceptional changes are referred to as mutant genes or mutations, and mutations are regarded as the raw materials from which evolutionary changes are compounded—by natural selection, by the process of sexual reproduction, or by other agencies. Mutations are, accordingly, changes induced ultimately by the environment, but the properties of a mutant are dependent on the nature of the gene that made the change, rather than on the environmental agency which acted as the trigger that set off the change.

Environment and the Manifestation of Heredity

Heredity, the constellation of genes, that is, the genotype, brings about the development of the organism by imposing specific patterns on the assimilated food materials derived from the environment. The interaction of heredity and environment makes the development of the organism pass through a succession of stages, from fertilization, through growth, reproduction, and old age, to death. At any stage the outcome of the development depends on the genotype and on the succession of environments which the developing organism has encountered up to that stage. The appearance, the structure, and the functional state which the body has at a given moment constitute its phenotype. The phenotype of a person changes continuously through life as his development proceeds. The changes in the manifestation of heredity in the phenotype contrast with the relative stability of the genotype. But it should be understood that the relative stability of the genotype is a dynamic one—the genes are "stable" not because they are isolated from the environment, which they are not, but because they reproduce themselves faithfully.

The phenotype of a person is at any given moment determined by his genotype plus his life history. The question of whether a given "trait" of an individual, such as his eye color, state of health, musical ability, or good or bad behavior, is determined by heredity or by environment is, thus, pointless. The question so stated results from the old confusion of biological heredity with legal inheritance. All traits arise in the process of living, which implies a heredity and a succession of environments. An eye color presupposes an eye, well-being or disease have no meaning without an organism which can or cannot contract certain diseases or suffer certain breakdowns, and benevolent and malevolent behavior imply the existence of a person who can discriminate between good and evil.

The so-called "nature-nurture," or heredity-environment, problem must be stated very carefully to be meaningful. The problem concerns *differences* between individuals or populations. Some people have blue and others brown eyes, some enjoy good health while others suffer from various infirmities, some can create or enjoy good music and others feel no interest in it, some are desirable members of society and others are outlaws. It is reasonable to inquire to what extent the observed *differences* in phenotypes are due to the existing variety of human genotypes and to the diversity of the environments in which people live.

There is not one nature-nurture problem, but many. To put it more precisely, what must be studied is the variation observed in a given characteristic among human beings in general, or among members of certain human populations. The part played in this variation by the existence of a diversity of human genotypes may then be evaluated and compared with the part played by the existing diversity of environments. The results obtained will be valid only for the characteristic or trait studied, for the population examined, and for the time and place when and where the examination is made.

For example, the relative importance of heredity is, taking mankind as a whole, probably greater in the variability of eye colors and skin colors than in the variability of height or weight. But it does not follow that skin color is always more strictly hereditary than height. Indeed, skin colors vary widely among the inhabitants of Virginia —from very pale to black. These wide variations are largely due to heredity, to the presence of genes of European and of African origin among the inhabitants of this state. The degree of variation in skin color is relatively much smaller among the inhabitants of a village in Norway, or of a village in central Africa, the populations of which are of more uniform racial origins. In this lesser variation the relative importance of the environmental component, the tanning effect of exposure to sunlight, is much greater than it is in Virginia. In general, if the environment in which a population lives is made constant, the phenotypic variation observed will be due to genotypic diversity. Conversely, making the population genotypically uniform results in the observed variation being environmental in origin.

Controlling the Phenotype

All human traits and qualities result from the interaction of heredity and environment in the process of living. This statement applies with equal force to the so-called physical traits and to the so-called psychic, behavioral, or cultural traits of persons and populations. Its applicability to the latter category of traits is frequently and vehemently challenged. To many people the idea that heredity enters as one of the determinants of the intellectual and emotional life of human beings is intensely distasteful. This distaste has two causes. First, there is no question that over-valuation of heredity and undervaluation of environment in human development has been, and is being used as a specious reason for bias, oppression, and cruelty of man to man. Suffice it to recall that it was this kind of prostitution of biology which was employed by the Nazis as justification for their crimes. Second, to many people heredity seems a sinister force which suddenly emerges mysteriously to inflict blows of physical or mental illness on the innocent. Along with this idea goes the equally mistaken one that a hereditary disease is an incurable disease, that hereditary traits cannot be influenced or modified by the environment, and therefore that traits which are susceptible of being modified or improved are, hence, not hereditary. All these misconceptions give rise to the notion that a biological inheritance of human psychic traits is incompatible with personal freedom.

Modern biology would have earned its keep if it did nothing else but show that these fears are unfounded, and biology certainly has done this. There is no such thing as a purely inherited or a purely environmental trait, since all traits arise during the process of development of a person who has a certain genotype *and* who lives in a certain environment. The degree to which the phenotypic manifestation of human heredity, or of the heredity of any biological species, can be predicted and controlled depends to a considerable extent upon our knowledge and understanding of the developmental processes involved.

How vast the possibilities in this field are can be seen from the steady progress of medicine and hygiene, the applied biological sciences that devise methods for the management of the human phenotype. Obviously it is the phenotypes of men and women whom we meet, and of men and women everywhere, that are of most concern to us in practice. Nevertheless, to control the phenotype we cannot ignore or underestimate the importance of the genotype, because different genotypes demand different environments to produce optimal phenotypes. When you consult your physician you expect him to prescribe such modifications of your environment as may be needed to enable your own genotype to give rise to a phenotype which you and other people consider satisfactory. The carriers of different genotypes often require different treatments. The meaning of the expression "hereditary disease" should now be clear. A disease is said to be hereditary when persons with a certain kind of genotype suffer in environments in which carriers of "normal" hereditary constitutions enjoy reasonable well-being.

As far as curability is concerned, there is no difference in principle between hereditary and nonhereditary diseases and malformations. The chances that, in a given environment, a person will contract a contagious disease or a degenerative ailment, as well as the symptoms with which a disease will manifest itself, are determined by the genotype. While all humans are susceptible, more or less, to such infections as malaria or syphilis, or to such diseases as senile degeneration of the circulatory system, for example, only persons who are carriers of certain genotypes are more susceptible to disorders such as diabetes than are other people.

Certain human genotypes require special environments to produce optimal phenotypes. Thus, hereditary diabetes is relieved by regular injections of insulin, which a normal body produces for itself. An incurable disease, whether hereditary or not, is one which is not relieved by any known environment. It should, however, be kept in mind that new environments are constantly being created by human ingenuity. New diets, new drugs, new living conditions, new educational systems are constantly being invented and introduced. Some, or most, human genotypes react to these new environments by producing desirable phenotypes. This is, in fact, the criterion which distinguishes good environments from bad ones, except that some environments may be good for some genotypes and bad for others.

Once the meaning of heredity is clearly understood, there should be no difficulty in accepting the proposition that man's intellectual and emotional life is conditioned by his genotype. This is self-evident on the species level, and is easily demonstrable on the individual level. The experiments of Yerkes and others have shown very clearly that the possibilities of acquisition of humanlike patterns of behavior are severely limited even in the great apes, not to speak of other animals lower on the scale. To be a man one has to have a human genotype, and an ape genotype will not do regardless of any amount of training and of any known environmental influences.

Heredity as a Basis of Culture

The whole subject of inheritance is wonderful.
CHARLES DARWIN

Biological and Cultural Evolutions

The biological uniqueness of man lies in the fact that the human species alone has evolved culture. The appearance of culture signified the beginning of a hitherto nonexistent type of evolutionary development—the evolution of culture or human evolution proper. The date of this event is uncertain; it may have taken place from half a million to more than a million years ago. In any case the humanness of man arose gradually rather than overnight. The significance of this event is comparable with that of a much earlier event, the origin of life from inanimate matter, which happened perhaps two billion years ago. The appearance of life, of self-reproduction, was the beginning of a new type of evolution, biological evolution. Cultural evolution was added to biological evolution, just as biological evolution was superimposed upon the evolution of matter, cosmic evolution. The beginning of cosmic evolution is now placed by physicists at about five billion years ago. In neither case has the new evolution replaced or abolished the old; cosmic evolution continued after the appearance of life, and both cosmic and biological evolutions went on following the emergence of man. Nevertheless, the beginnings of the cosmic, biological, and human evolutions are crucial events in the history of Creation. In producing life, cosmic evolution overcame its own bounds; in giving rise to man, biological evolution transcended itself. Human evolution may yet ascend to a superhuman level.

Kluckhohn has defined culture as "the total life-way of a people, the social legacy the individual acquires from his group." An alternative definition is "Culture is the learned portion of human behavior." The key word in this last definition is "learned," as it draws a clear distinction between biological and cultural heredity. Indeed, the mechanisms of transmission of biological heredity do not differ appreciably in man from those in other organisms which reproduce by sexual unions. Biological heredity is transmitted by genes; consequently it is handed down exclusively from parents to their children and other direct descendants. Culture is transmitted by teaching and learning. At least in principle, "the social legacy" can be transmitted by anybody to anyone, regardless of biological descent.

Man may be said to have two heredities, a biological one and a cultural one; all other organisms have only the biological one. But this statement rather oversimplifies the actual situation and may prove misleading. It is important to realize that biological heredity and culture, the inborn and the learned behavior, are not independent or isolated entities. They are interacting processes. The acquisition and maintenance of culture by learning is possible only owing to the biological organization with which the human species is genetically endowed. Culture is said to be "superorganic." But the superorganic stands in a relation of interdependence with the organic. Human evolution is a singular product of interaction between biology and culture.

Cultural Conditioning

A quaint medieval belief had it that infants who do not hear spoken any human language come to talk in ancient Hebrew, which is the language of God. The basis of this legend is evidently the naive idea that there is such a thing as an innate or intrinsic language of mankind, which one may come to know without learning. Of course there is no such language. The language or languages which a person speaks are not contained in his genes; they must be acquired by learning in childhood or in later years. No less naive are the attempts to explain various cultural characteristics, and even all human behavior, as biologically determined ways to satisfy the bodily functions and drives of the human animal. Modern cultural anthropology has shown very clearly that there is no "culture" planted by nature in the genes of any members of the human species. A human individual acquires only gradually, by means of the processes of socialization and acculturation, the habits, skills, and beliefs which integrate him into his society. Socialization and acculturation consist of conditioning and learning; they confer upon a person a competence to deal with his human and his physical environment.

An infant is born with a genotype which makes him receptive to conditioning by other human beings with whom he is associated—parents, relatives, playmates, teachers, and, directly or indirectly, most or all members of the society or the group to which he belongs. Children isolated from contacts with other humans grow up having only a physical resemblance to human beings; human mind and human behavior are products mainly of the accommodation the individual makes to the habits, standards, tastes, opinions, beliefs, feelings, and values imposed by the community. In the words of Herskovits: "This is because every human being is born into a group whose customs and beliefs are established before he arrives on the scene. Through the learning process he acquires these customs and beliefs; and he learns his cultural lessons so well that much of his behavior in later years takes the form of automatic responses to the cultural stimuli with which he is presented."

Culturally induced traits make human beings behave predictably in many situations. Many such traits are so constant in members of a given culture that members of that culture take those traits for granted and only notice their absence when they meet people brought up in cultures different from their own. The behavior of such people may seem, therefore, baffling and even perverse. It should be noted in this connection that "culture" as used by anthropologists signifies not only science, art, philosophy, and religion, but also such practices of daily life as ways of preparing and eating food, of sleeping, of taking care of children, of personal cleanliness, and so on. Thus it comes about that millions of people in the Middle East feel disgusted at the very thought of eating pork, while millions of people in the West consider ham or pork sausage a delicacy. There is no need to assume the existence of genes which would make one like or dislike pork; it is all a matter of conditioning or habit. Similarly, people who are used to sleeping in beds feel most uncomfortable sleeping in hammocks as people in tropical America do, and vice versa. Again this is a matter of training, not of genes. In some of these cultural traits retraining is possible, with some effort. At the cost of some uncomfortable nights, this writer has now learned to sleep very comfortably either in a bed or a hammock.

Language

Language is a most important product of culture and, at the same time, is its vehicle, facilitating the perpetuation and further development of culture. Most animals are able to produce and to perceive sounds, and the different kinds of sounds which an animal can produce are frequently put to use in establishing communication between individuals of its species. The "songs" of crickets, katydids, and cicadas play a role in helping the two sexes find each other. In birds and in mammals, sounds may express emotions, and may be used to warn strangers away from territories already occupied by representatives of the same species, to attract one's kind to sources of food, or to give the alarm when danger is approaching. Human language is a phenomenon of a different sort. Human speech consists of words which are symbols for various objects, actions, and thoughts. Herskovits defines human language as "a system of arbitrary vocal symbols by which members of a social group cooperate and interact, and by means of which the learning process is effectuated and a given way of life achieves both continuity and change."

The capacity for using language of this kind is peculiarly human, and is found in animals other than man only in the most rudimentary forms. This capacity is given by the human biological nature, i.e., by the human genotype. Any normal child can learn any human language apparently quite easily, although some adults encounter great difficulties when they try to learn foreign languages. Which language one speaks is a matter of culture, but the ability to speak some language is a matter of genes. Moreover, although the great majority of human beings possess genotypes which make them able to think in symbols and to express their thoughts in speech, there are those who lack such genotypes. Here belong the various forms of congenital idiocy which are due to defective heredity. Substitution of a single gene in the sex cell from which the individual develops makes the difference between a normal human being and an amaurotic idiot. A change in a single gene can so alter the course of the development of the organism that, instead of a normal child who easily absorbs the elements of culture, there is produced a wretched being, unable to respond to the socializing influences of his human environment.

The possibility has been suggested that some features of a given language, though they can be mastered by outsiders, may be conditioned by physical characteristics of the racial groups which have developed this language. Indeed, almost every language has special sounds, phonemes, which are absent in many other languages, and which other people often find hard to imitate. Thus the English *th* phoneme is awkward for many continental Europeans, some Russian phonemes are difficult for English speakers, and the "click" sounds of the languages of the natives of South Africa are perplexing to most other people. The hypothesis that these phonemes may be related to some peculiarities in the sound-producing organs of different races cannot be dismissed out-of-hand, although it certainly has never been proved. It is mentioned here chiefly to stress the fact that there is no incompatibility between genetic and cultural conditioning. A phoneme may be due to both, and though anyone can learn a "click," at least as a child, some people may conceivably find doing so easier than others.

Propagation of Culture

It has already been pointed out that the transmission of culture occurs by a means that is entirely different from that which transfers biological heredity. The latter is handed down from parents to children at the moment of conception, by means of the genes in the sex cells. Culture is continuously acquired by a person throughout life. Transmission and acquisition of culture occurs by conditioning, teaching, guidance, precept, indoctrination, learning, imitation, and finally by conscious choice. Cultural traits can be transmitted potentially to any number of persons regardless of descent relationships. Language is the most ancient and powerful means of propagating culture. The invention of writing, and later of printing, has made the dissemination of culture vastly more efficient. Transmission of culture can now occur through space, between persons who live in different parts of the world. It can occur through time, from persons long dead to living ones. Founders of religions, philosophers, poets, scientists, artists, inventors, intellectual and political leaders exert strong influence, for good or for evil, centuries and millenia after their deaths. Most of mankind today are directly or indirectly influenced by Christian civilization, and particularly by its branch known as Western civilization. These civilizations perpetuate systems of ideas and of ideals arrived at some two thousand years ago in Palestine, in Greece, Rome, and in other parts of the Mediterranean world.

Acquired cultural characteristics are transmitted; acquired bodily characteristics are not. Acquired bodily characteristics die with the body which acquired them. The body is a by-product of the self-reproduction of genes, not the other way round as wrongly supposed by Lamarck and his followers. There is no inherent mechanism of replication or reproduction in culture traits. This makes culture both more easily transmittible and more easily modifiable than is biological heredity. All the inventions, scientific findings, musical compositions, and literary works which mankind now living treasures and enjoys were created by relatively few individuals through their personal efforts. Galileo, Leonardo, Newton, Beethoven, Faraday, Shakespeare, Darwin, Dostoevsky, to name only a handful of the more recent originators of our precious cultural heritage, exert great and enduring influence on millions of people. In cultural fields, more than anywhere else, the many owe much to the few. The splendor of the arts and the advances of science and technology are often due to astonishingly small numbers of persons. Biological evolution is, in this sense, a far less efficient process.

Considered biologically, culture is, of course, a part of the environment in which the development of a person is taking place. Indeed the "environment" consists not only of physical variables such as temperature, humidity, light, quantity and quality of the food, but includes also the interrelations which are established between individuals of one species and of other species living in the same habitat. Culture is, however, a nearly exclusively human phenomenon, and as such it deserves to be regarded as the third group of determinants of human personality, along with heredity and environment.

Variations Within a Culture

The processes of socialization and acculturation render it certain that every normal person can function as a member of the community into which he is born. As Benedict wrote in her *Patterns of Culture:* "From the moment of his [the child's] birth the customs into which he is born shape his experience and behavior. By the time he can talk, he is the little creature of his culture, and by the time he is grown and able to take part in its activities, its habits are his habits, its beliefs his beliefs, its impossibilities his impossibilities." Every American or European wears clothing of a certain type, and regards appearing naked in public places as indecent. But an Amazonian Indian goes naked, and to him clothing, other than a loincloth, is a nuisance. Every American learns to use a fork and a spoon for eating; every Chinese is adept with chopsticks. In most cultures eating human flesh is a loathsome crime, but in some it is a heroic act and a source of power and authority.

But it should be self-evident that within the bounds of each cultural pattern different individuals are not merely allowed but indeed are forced to develop variations in personality and behavior. Kluckhohn and Murray distinguish four groups of personality determinants: constitutional, group membership, role, and situational. Constitutional determinants include, apart from sex and age, the individual genotype which makes one individual react differently from another individual in similar socializing influences. Group membership refers to the fact that most persons live amongst, and hence identify themselves with, either Hottentots or Eskimos, Americans or Russians, or whatever the case may be. Accordingly, they are expected to behave and even to feel like a Hottentot, an Eskimo, an American, or a Russian usually does. Within each group, different individuals choose, or are assigned to play, different roles. There are craftsmen, farmers, aristocrats, tinkers, tailors, soldiers, and sailors. This again imposes or favors certain behavior patterns, and often leads to identification with and loyalty to the chosen or assigned role. And, finally, every person finds himself in a situation that is, to some extent, unlike that of any other person, and these unique situations come and go as long as life endures. Hence no two persons, not even members of a pair of identical twins, are ever exactly alike.

The existence of intracultural variations is clearly of the greatest importance for the success of a culture as a whole and for the welfare of the society which is the possessor of this culture. In fact, some nonliterate cultures permit a relative uniformity of personalities among their members, while in advanced cultures the variety of functions to be performed or roles to be played is very great. In bringing about intracultural diversity of personality and behavior, constitutional or genetic variables are most important, and yet they are given a minimum of, if any, attention by some anthropologists and sociologists. Assertions have even been made that the existence of genetically controlled personality variations is doubtful, or not proven, or of no particular importance compared to environmental and cultural influences. Such assertions can only be explained by the general lack of comprehension of the true nature of heredity. The problem here involved would appear less intricate, and certainly would provoke less passionate partisanship, if it was more generally realized that genetic conditioning does not necessarily imply a fixity of any trait. Still less does it exclude the influence of environment on the trait concerned, or dash the hope of being able to control human phenotypes.

The Nature-Nurture Problem

A detailed discussion of the nature-nurture problem as it applies to human behavior would be out of place here. Some examples of genotypic variations which influence psychic traits, and consequently the responses of individuals to cultural experiences, may nevertheless be given to illustrate the relationship between biological heredity and culture. The existence of such genotypic variations is proven beyond reasonable doubt.

The clearest evidence of genetic conditioning of psychic traits comes from studies of grossly pathological disturbances, which lead to mental deficiencies or disorders. A classic example is the disorder called phenylpyruvic oligophrenia. Such afflicted persons excrete in their urine a substance known as phenylpyruvic acid. Associated with this abnormality of metabolism is a severe mental deficiency ranging from imbecility to idiocy. The metabolic deficiency is due to the presence, in a homozygous condition, of a double dosage of a certain recessive gene. Another recessive gene can produce juvenile amaurotic idiocy, which involves blindness, mental disintegration, and death before the advent of adolescence.

There are probably dozens, and possibly hundreds, of other genes in man which produce various forms of mental deficiencies that have been studied less rigorously. The evidence for the existence of these genes comes chiefly from comparisons of the incidence of such deficiencies in identical and fraternal twins. Identical twins carry similar genotypes, while the genetic endowments of fraternal twins are, on the average, as different as those of brothers and sisters who are not twins. Among identical twins, if one of the twins shows a mental deficiency then the co-twin also shows it in over 90 percent of the cases examined. Among fraternal twins, the frequency of such "concordance" among members of the twin pairs is only around 50 percent. The higher frequency of concordance among identical twins shows that many forms of mental deficiency have a genetic basis. But the fact that the concordance is less than 100 percent shows either that some cases of mental deficiency are due to environmental accidents, or that the abnormal genotypes do not produce the deficiency in some environments.

Mental deficiency makes the afflicted persons intractable to the socializing influences of their cultural environment. They cannot learn simple things which a normal child learns easily, or do so only with great difficulty. But it is not necessary to use pathological traits, like phenylpyruvic oligophrenia or mental deficiencies, to demonstrate the genetic conditioning of human behavior. The reason why pathological traits are so often used in genetic studies is that, for technical reasons, they are more amenable for such studies.

Consider, however, simply two "normal" boys, one of whom is tall, muscular, and conforming to the popular notion of "good looks," while the other is short, fat, and ungainly. There is no doubt that such physical differences are in part genetically conditioned, although, of course, they are influenced also by environment. Now, the first boy is likely to be successful in sports, popular with his playmates, and confident in his manner and conduct. He may develop into a man of action. The second boy is likely to avoid competitive sports, grow to be more reserved, be inclined towards solitude and interested in scholarship and thought rather than in action. The fact that the careers of both boys are dependent upon the cultural practices of the society into which they are born does not in the least contradict the partial genetic conditioning of their careers. The genotype conditions the behavior within a certain environment and within a certain cultural framework. Nor does the hypothesis of genetic conditioning require that all athletic boys become men of action and all fat boys become scholars. The genetic and environmental variables are too numerous for this.

An even more thought-provoking situation has been disclosed by the studies of criminality in twins. Different investigators in different countries have examined pairs of identical and fraternal twins for criminality. The data of all the investigators agrees fairly well in showing that if one of the twins had a criminal record, his co-twin had such a record more often if the twins were identical than if they were fraternal. From these simple and straightforward results, some writers saw fit to conclude that criminality is hereditary, and is a "destiny" of the persons afflicted with such a heredity. A further conclusion, rarely stated explicitly, but often implied or insinuated, is that crime cannot be controlled by social measures and that society is not to blame for its existence. Other writers have attempted to discredit the data by all sorts of casuistry, since, according to them, crime is a social phenomenon and cannot have a biological basis.

The dispute is due to a misunderstanding and a misstatement of the problem. The data shows that in certain environments individuals with similar heredities tend to be more similar in behavior than individuals with different heredities. But it does not follow that possession of a certain genotype compels a person to enter upon a career of crime. Nor does it follow that persons with other heredities would resist temptation if they were placed in the environments in which the actual criminals grew and developed. Least of all can one conclude that social and educational measures would not have saved anybody from becoming a criminal. Criminality is not "intrinsic," since heredity does not ordain that its possessor will be a criminal. What heredity does do is merely to condition the reactions of a person to various environments. Whether a person so conditioned grows to be a criminal, a law-abiding citizen, or a saint depends upon the life experience of this person —his upbringing, education, opportunity, associations with other people—and good or bad luck.

At our present level of knowledge, no one can be sure how great are the relative roles of the genetic and of the environmental components in the variations of behavior observed among different persons in any culture. All that we can be sure of is that both components are involved to some extent. And yet, in the heat of the nature-nurture controversy, the importance of either one or the other component has frequently been denied or minimized. We have considered above some evidences of the effectiveness of the genetic component. It may now be desirable to look on the other side of the ledger, since some psychic traits, the inborn nature of which was almost taken for granted, proved on investigation to be actually due to conditioning.

Perhaps the most spectacular results of this kind have been obtained by Cantril and his school of psychologists. They constructed rooms of irregular shapes, with tilting floors and ceilings, and nonrectangular walls. When, however, an observer looks into such a room through an observation hole, the image given on his retina by its walls is like that given by an ordinary rectangular room, and so the observer sees a room of a familiar shape. He can be made to realize that the room is not rectangular, and to see its real shape, if he is made to use it and to act within it. Our ability to see things is, then, not just a matter of having healthy eyes. The evidences of our senses are ordered in our minds by experience and conditioning, and to see an unfamiliar world as it really is may require new experience and reconditioning.

Differences between Cultures

The inception of culture became possible when our prehuman ancestors began to evolve genotypes more similar to our own than to those of our more remote animal ancestors. Culture is, therefore, a product of the genotype with which our species is endowed. But here one must guard against an error, which is all the more dangerous because it is subtle and easily overlooked. Namely, it has just been stated that the human genotype has made culture possible; but it does not follow that a culture of any particular kind, or even of any kind, is an inevitable consequence of the existence of the human genotype. The gap between potentiality and actuality is often discouragingly wide. The genotype of the human species is a necessary, but not a sufficient, condition for cultural development. The evolution of culture is a long historical process, the causes of which lie mostly within the culture itself, rather than in its biological substratum. Few problems in science are more important and intriguing than that of the causes of cultural development. The approach to this problem is facilitated by the fact that the human species has evolved not one but many different cultures and subcultures. The different cultures can, then, be compared, and attempts can be made to analyze the origins of the differences and similarities between them. This is being done with remarkable success by cultural anthropologists. The observational material already accumulated is impressively large, and the analytical schemes and the working hypotheses proposed are thought-provoking and stimulating for further research. Most biologists have been guilty of paying insufficient attention to this material and to its analysis. This has caused great harm to the understanding of all aspects of human evolution.

It is self-evident that "culture" does not exist apart from the human individuals who are its carriers. All the libraries in the world would be useless without the people who read the books, and all music would be worthless without those who perform and appreciate it. Similarly, in some parts of the Middle East, women veil their faces because there it is considered indecent for a woman's face to be seen by a male other than her husband. In recent years, however, this custom is beginning to disappear in some countries where it used to be prevalent, because people are accepting the exposure of the face as proper and respectable.

The way of life of a society shows an internal cohesion. Comparative studies of many kinds of societies, both nonliterate and advanced, have disclosed that the beliefs, customs, and practices of a group of people usually hold together as related parts of a whole. A durable culture shows a certain patterning or integration of its components. A change in one part of a culture may, then, require correlated changes in the whole pattern to make the system workable. The importance of this integration has been shown in a series of unpremeditated experiments. The contacts of primitive societies with Western civilization have in many instances resulted in a breakdown of the former and even in the extinction of the tribes which formed these societies. The breakdown was caused by attempts, frequently honest and well-meaning, on the part of the Western "civilizers" to alter drastically some aspects of the way of life of the subject populations without harmonizing these alterations with other aspects. The mental health and happiness of a people, both as individuals and as a group, is often dependent on the possession of a coherent cultural pattern.

But why have peoples in different parts of the world evolved different cultures, and why do they continue to follow different ways of life? This is evidently a part of the nature-nurture problem mentioned above. The differences between groups of people integrated in different societies, just as the differences between persons within any one of such groups, may be due either to heredity, or to environment, or to a combination of both. When discussing cultures, it is also useful to keep in mind the distinction between the physical environment (climates, soils, geographic conditions in general) and the cultural environments proper (contacts with other peoples, the history of the culture itself).

Arguments and disputes concerning the origins and maintenance of cultures have been rife for centuries, and no agreement is yet in sight. This is due in part to the insufficiency of scientifically reliable data, in part to emotional biases involved, and in part to widespread misunderstanding of relevant biological and sociological concepts. The brief discussion that follows obviously does not aspire to give a solution to the problem; it merely aims at clarifying some issues about which a biologist may have some competence.

The Racist Hypothesis

Even men of powerful intellect are apt to allow one idea, or one method of approach, to make them unreceptive, or even hostile, to all others. It was the subtle and sophisticated thinker Gobineau who wrote, almost exactly a century ago, his *Essay on the Inequality of Human*

Races. Race pride and race prejudice have existed since time immemorial; indulgence of these emotions is the cheapest way to gratify one's vanity. What was new in Gobineau was the pseudoscientific foundation which he invented for race prejudice. The only civilization worthy of the name is, according to Gobineau, Western civilization. It has been created, developed, and maintained by just one race—the blue-eyed, blond Nordics. All other races of mankind are incapable not only of advancing but even of making use of civilization. To make things worse, Gobineau's Nordics are only minority groups, aristocratic elites, in certain, "select" countries of Western Europe. They are being swamped by intermarriage with inferior races and classes. Mankind is approaching a biological and cultural twilight.

Francis Galton, an outstanding biologist and statistician, was one of the pioneers in the studies of human heredity and the founder of the eugenics movement. Nevertheless, he accepted the essentials of Gobineau's views, and restated them in terms of Darwinian evolutionary theories. According to Galton, "The instincts and faculties of different men and races differ in a variety of ways almost as profoundly as those of animals in different cages of the Zoological Gardens." The history of mankind is, then, essentially the competition and struggle of races and classes with different genetic endowments. Just as among animals, the genetically fittest come out on top, to govern, to command, and to create and enjoy cultural values. The genetically less fit are born to obey, or else "go to the wall."

Racist interpretations of culture and of history have

been very popular for a century, and still remain so in many circles. They have been developed in numerous books and in the popular press, and have influenced the policy of many governments. Their acceptance was compulsory in Nazi Germany. Their restatement in terms of modern biology has been given in a recent book by Darlington. His theory of culture is effectively summarized thus: "The genetic sequence of civilization . . . is that the genetically fixed capacities of individual men influence their beliefs and their social behavior; secondly, having done so, they in turn influence the groups in which the individuals will mate; and thirdly, the mating group selects and concentrates the genetic capacities of individual men. By this circular sequence we can now see that a differentiation of the society is established on the genetic basis, of which the people concerned are unconscious."

The trouble with the race theory of culture is that it simply fails to explain anything. No correlation has ever been established between the contents of a culture and any physical or physiological characteristics of its possessors. Quite the contrary, cultures have again and again been successfully taken over, as a whole or in part, by people of quite different racial stocks. And conversely, the same population can and has often changed its culture drastically during the course of its history with or without outside influence. After 1852, Japan rapidly absorbed much of European culture, and quite successfully blended it with its indigenous cultural pattern, so successfully in fact that it caused considerable difficulty to the original possessors of this culture in the years immediately following Pearl Harbor. But the Japanese have not become members of the Caucasian race—even though Hitler did propose to make them "honorary Aryans."

Less than two thousand years ago, the ancestors of most modern Americans and Europeans were barbarians eking out a rough and precarious existence in the forests and swamps of northern Europe. But these barbarians responded magnificently when they were given an opportunity to borrow foreign cultures developed by the rather different peoples who inhabited the lands around the eastern part of the Mediterranean Sea. Successful cultural reconditioning can now be observed any day in the large universities in such centers as New York, London, Paris, or Moscow, which attract students from all over the world. At least some of these students become culturally more similar to each other and to their hosts than they are to some of their own biological relatives who have stayed at home. Evidence that cultural patterns are determined by the genes is utterly lacking. What evidence there is rather contradicts this hypothesis. The greatest fallacy of the racist hypothesis is, then, its failure to take into account the adaptive importance of the behavioral plasticity in man.

Hypotheses of Genetic Uniformity

Perhaps partly as a reaction against the crudities of biological racism, the tendency became strengthened among some anthropologists to ignore the existence of genetic differences between persons and populations altogether. An example of this is the statement of Mead: "We are working with two sets of variables, the biological equipment of human beings and the historical forms within which this equipment has been patterned. We therefore 'hold human nature constant' and assume, for the present, that human nature may be regarded as similar for Bushmen, Hottentots, Americans of 1941, etc. Were we not to do so, it would be impossible to conduct such a series of experiments." The "experiments" consist of attempts to study the origin of the personality differences in various cultures. In many ways Hottentots and Americans do behave alike, but in other ways they behave differently. Although human nature is supposedly uniform everywhere, nevertheless there do exist cultural differences between groups of people.

The culture which a group of people possesses tends to maintain its identity and continuity generation after generation. Far from being due to biological heredity as the racists assume, this continuity of culture attests to the remarkable plasticity and malleability of human behavior as shaped in the processes of socialization and acculturation discussed above. People learn to behave as, and to identify themselves with, Hottentots, or with Frenchmen, or Japanese, or Americans. They pick up and incorporate the cultural pattern of their group, which is organized to yield a way of life adaptive to a given physical and social environment. The complex of learned behavior and tradition which is called culture is, thus, transmitted in its entirety from generation to generation. But a child of Japanese parents may learn to be an American, and an

American may take on the French cultural tradition. Furthermore, the cultural tradition itself undergoes changes; with culture, as with biological heredity, continuity does not preclude transformation.

Comparative studies of acculturation as it occurs in various nonliterate as well as in advanced societies have thrown much light on the mechanisms of transmitting culture. Childhood experiences, particularly those of early childhood and infancy, have proved to be extremely important in shaping the personality as it manifests itself in adult life. In these studies cultural anthropology has been greatly influenced by the psychoanalytic theories of Freud and his followers.

Freud was certainly one of the great men of our time, and truly a discoverer of a new field of knowledge, the existence of which, although discerned before him, had not been described even in the quasi-scientific terms in which Freud stated his discoveries. New is the discovery of the vast field of the unconscious which man has been shown to carry in his psyche. The unconscious drives, which a biologist must assume to be genotypically controlled, interact with the conscious "ego" and with the requirements of the social milieu. It is this interaction that is responsible for the formation of the personality. The emotional cravings of infants, including infant sexuality, are forerunners of the drives which appear in different forms and which play different roles in adult life. These cravings and drives of infancy and childhood are differently channelled in different cultures by means of the frustrations, constraints, pressures, and encouragements inflicted on growing children by their parents and other members of the society into which they are born. The resulting personality structures become and remain different during the whole lifetime.

It would be presumptuous for a biologist to undertake to distinguish between the grain and the chaff in the great observational and theoretical harvest gathered by Freud and his followers. However, Freud's findings and conclusions impinge on biology in many ways. Freud has refused to consider the possible role of the genetic differences between people in the formation of their personalities. This refusal was perhaps legitimate in his case. Having discovered a whole new world, he could afford for a time to use hypotheses which were frank oversimplifications. But the justification of continuing to use such hypotheses may well be questioned at present. The origins of the unconscious urges and drives of the human infant are not explained; their existence is simply taken for granted. These drives are certainly variable from individual to individual, and this variability may well be partly, or even largely, under genetic control.

Psychoanalytic techniques have been, and still continue to be, used chiefly as a form of curative and preventive medicine dealing with neuroses and other mental disturbances. The observations, and the theories derived from them, are based mainly on this therapeutic and clinical work. This may explain the lack of attention on the part of the Freudians to some important and fascinating implications of their work. What are the evolutionary origins of the unconscious drives of the id, of the super-ego, which they discover and investigate? These factors play an unexpectedly large role in shaping human lives. A biologist cannot fail to ask: What is the adaptive significance of these factors in the biological success or failure of persons and populations? What factors have promoted the formation of the id in the process of evolution from animal to man? The breakdowns and neuroses with which the psychoanalysts deal in their therapeutic practice are, after all, miscarriages of the normal developmental processes. These developmental processes must be so conditioned by the human genotype that a healthy personality is formed in most instances. But is this conditioning alike in everybody?

There can be scarcely any doubt that the psychoanalytic theory has been misapplied in some of the attempts to explain cultural differences. Very learned books have been written which claim to have found "clues" to the understanding of national characteristics in child-rearing practices and the experiences of infants in the respective nations. Thus, the "clues" to the American national character lie in the way American infants are handled, in the vast quantities of cow's milk they consume, and, chiefly, in the "rejection of the father." The "clue" to the Japanese character is the too early and too severe toilet training of Japanese infants. And the peculiar features of the Russian character are induced in Russian infants chiefly by the prolonged and tight swaddling, which conveys to them the idea that a strong governmental authority is desirable.

This "diaper anthropology" is, in a way, a mirror image

of biological racism. It rejects biological determinism, but manages to erect a determinism just as rigid, and, if anything, even more gratuitous. Granted, there is good evidence that childhood experiences are important in the development of a person. But there is no valid evidence that the "clue" to the character of a whole nation can be found in its prevailing techniques of handling its infants. This is already highly unlikely on biological grounds. The development of the adaptively very important part of the human phenotype called "personality" cannot be credited to environmental agencies as irrelevant to the needs of a person during most of his life span as swaddling or toilet training of an infant. We hope to show that the development patterns of the genotypes commonly found in a race or a species are molded in the process of evolution and controlled by natural selection. These developmental patterns may be fixed rather rigidly, or may be sensitive to environmental variations, whichever condition is more advantageous for the survival and reproduction of their carriers. Biological racists believe them to be fixed by heredity. "Diaper anthropologists" share the belief in fixity, but they let child-rearing practices do the fixing. We shall argue that an essential feature of human evolution which has made our species unique has been the establishment of a genetically controlled plasticity of personality traits. This plasticity has made man educable and has made human culture and society possible.

Conclusion

It was the fond hope and ardent belief of eighteenth-century Enlightenment that a man at birth was a *tabula rasa*, an empty receptacle. Upbringing and environment poured into this receptacle the contents which formed the individual's personality. At the same time men are, by their Nature, inclined to be good, virtuous, and endowed with Reason. If only Reason were allowed to develop itself fully, and if everybody obeyed its commands, then everybody would be happy and all evil would vanish from the world. Stupidity and wickedness are due to the unnatural structure of a society which makes men deviate from their natural goodness.

Our own age has inherited this myth from the Age of Enlightenment. On the whole, the biological and social sciences support the hope which this myth implies. Biological racism and "diaper anthropology" are just aberrations of scientific thought. But a better knowledge of nature, and particularly of human nature, helps to correct some of the myth's fanciful aspects. Man is not born a *tabula rasa*. Human nature is variable; in fact no two men are alike by nature. An individual learns to be the kind of person which he eventually becomes. He can learn to perform any one of a great many different kinds of social functions, and hence can develop into any one of a great many different kinds of persons. Which one he does become depends on the society in which he lives and on his genetic endowment. In any culture there occurs a process of socialization, in which the individual is trained to react to stimuli which occur in his environment in ways approved of or at least tolerated in that culture. The term "socialization" is applied chiefly to the training received in childhood, but obviously this process never ends, since no behavior pattern is acceptable indefinitely. The role which an individual plays changes with age and with altering environmental situations; this makes it necessary for every person to react adaptively to every situation as it arises.

We need not assume that human nature is similar in Hottentots and in Americans. We may reasonably doubt that it is. On the other hand, we do know that members of all nations and races are capable of creative response to different cultural influences. The ancestors of some people now possessing the most advanced of civilizations were uncouth barbarians only a few centuries ago. The descendants of the most advanced peoples of the past are lagging behind at present. Within less than a century there have been some remarkable changes in the "unchanging East." In our own day tremendous changes are going on all over the world, new kinds of cultures and cultural influences are emerging and old ones are passing away. It is not likely that all mankind is marching towards cultural uniformity. Perhaps this lack of uniformity is due in part to genotypic diversity. If so, we must be thankful that man has evolved genotypic diversity in the process of his evolution.

Who Is the Fittest?

For good nurture and education implant good constitutions, and these good constitutions taking root in a good education improve more and more, and this improvement affects the breed in man as in other animals. PLATO

Causes of Evolution

At some point early in the Ice Age, more than half a million but probably not more than a million years ago, there evolved a very odd species of mammal called man. This mammal walked, and even ran, erect. His anterior extremities, freed from walking duties, were hands capable of a variety of movements, and consequently of delicate operations. His brain was very large in relation to his body, and made him capable of abstract thought. This last ability made possible the development of language. Language facilitated the accumulation and transmission of a body of learned behavior and tradition known as culture. The influence of culture on the evolutionary pattern of mankind occurred, then, by way of biological causation.

The development of culture became the dominant evolutionary force in the human species. However, its inception and development became possible only because of that unique biological endowment, the human genotype. Human evolution is the outcome of interactions between biological and cultural factors. These interactions we must now attempt to examine.

We have seen that biological evolution is change in the heredity, that is, change in the genes, of populations or colonies of living organisms. Most biologists agree that such change can be brought about through the interaction of three principal causative agents. These are mutation, gene recombination, and selection. Mutation produces changes in the genes and variants of the gene structure; these are the raw materials of evolution. In those organisms which reproduce sexually, these variants are combined and recombined to form countless different genotypes.

Sexual reproduction is the superlatively effective mechanism which creates novel constellations of genes. In the higher organisms at least, it becomes much more important than mutation as a creator of new genotypes. The potentialities of this mechanism are truly immense. With 1,000 genes, each capable of mutating in 10 different ways, $10^{1,000}$ genotypes are possible. This number is vastly greater than the number of atoms in the entire universe. Obviously, only an infinitesimal fraction of the possible gene combinations are or can ever be realized anywhere in the world. And any one gene combination is unlikely to arise repeatedly. Every human being is, then, the carrier of a unique genotype. With the exception of identical twins, no two persons are at all likely to be genetically identical.

To be sure, it must be remembered that the inexhaustible variety of genotypes consists of the many different combinations of the relatively smaller number of variant gene structures (alleles) which originally arose by mutation. Should we conclude that the recombination of genes in the sexual process produces nothing really "new"? Some writers have drawn just this conclusion. It should be kept in mind, however, that a gene does not exert its effect on development independent of other genes. The development of an organism, especially that of higher animals, is the product of the interaction of all the genes which the organism possesses. Sexual reproduction is thus a creative process; it originates biological novelty.

Most important for an understanding of human evolution is a knowledge of the action of natural selection on human populations. The role played by selection in biological evolution was set forth by Darwin almost a century ago. Since then, much more has been learned about this force, but at the same time an extraordinary amount of confusion and misinformation has been spread, especially among nonbiologists, concerning this biological phenomenon. This is particularly true regarding selection on the human level, since here the biological confusion has become further compounded by the manifold misuse of biology for purposes of political propaganda. Certain basic considerations bearing upon selection must, accordingly, be stated before the nature and the limitations of this evolutionary factor in man can be understood.

Survival of the Fittest

Malthus, an English parson and an amateur sociologist, published in 1798 his *Essay on the Principles of Population,* and hereby started the controversy which rages unabated even now, a century and a half later. In 1838, Darwin "happened to read for amusement" the work of Malthus. Out of this "amusement" grew Darwin's original version of the theory of natural selection. Malthus had pointed out that more children are born than live to become adults, and Darwin saw that this is true of any biological species. No matter how fast or how slow the reproductive processes in a species are, the population sooner or later may grow to such an extent that it will outrun its food supply, and a part of the progeny in every generation will die out because of the "struggle for existence." Hunger, disease, and war are the "Malthusian checks" which keep the population's size within the bounds imposed by its environment.

Now, what determines which individuals survive and which fall by the wayside? To some extent this is a matter of chance or luck. However, individuals who are stronger, more agile, more clever, or better able to get along on less sustenance will survive more often than will weaklings and the exigent ones. Spencer called this the "survival of the fittest," and Darwin overlooked the subtle implication caused by the use of the superlative. In reality, the fit, and even some of the unfit, have a chance to survive. The survival of the fit, or even of the fittest, would, however, have no influence on the quality of subsequent generations unless the fitness of the survivors and the unfitness of the victims was at least partly conditioned by their respective heredities. Darwin has demonstrated that fitness indeed has an inheritable component. This being the case, the struggle seems to serve a noble purpose, which is the maintenance and improvement of the adaptation that the organism has made to its environment. In the long run, the improvement of the adaptedness results in the transformation of the organic forms—or in evolution.

In many ways, the tenor of the theory of natural selection suited the intellectual climate of the second half of the nineteenth century remarkably well. In an age believing in and profiting by machines, the theory supplied a mechanical explanation of evolution. With colonial empires abuilding and with imperial nations preparing to dispute each other's claims to world mastery, it was a comforting thought that when the strong exploit or oppress the weak they are merely obeying natural laws and striving towards "progress." When armies are on the march, it is a comfort for those staying at home to believe that "war is nature's pruning-hook."

It is not surprising, then, that Darwin's theory of natural selection was malappropriated and misused to serve base ends. From this arose the accusation that Darwin invented a theory of hatred and cruelty. The accusers failed, however, to take note that Darwin's theory was good biology which was perverted by others to support bad sociology. Surely a maker of knives is not necessarily responsible for the assassin who uses a knife to cut the throat of his victim. Darwin's theory supplies no warrant for brutality or inhumanity. Darwin himself was not responsible for the growth of the "social darwinism" which others attempted to graft onto his theory of biological evolution.

Fitness and Reproductive Success

Modern versions of the theory of natural selection are in a way simpler than the classical. In any one generation, the carriers of different genotypes make, on the average, unequal contributions to the hereditary endowment of succeeding generations. The mean contribution of the carriers of each genotype, or class of genotypes, relative to those carriers of other genotypes within the population, characterizes the Darwinian fitness, or the adaptive value, of the genotype. The fit genotypes, and, by extension, the fit phenotypes, are those which transmit efficiently their genes to future generations. The less fit genotypes transmit their genes less effectively; the unfit ones leave little or no surviving, reproductively competent progeny.

At first sight the distinction between the classical and the modern variants of the theory of natural selection may seem to be of no great consequence. In reality the difference is important. The classical "fittest" was the lusty, implacable conqueror in the never-ending struggle for existence with his fellows and with other creatures. Fitness required vigor, power, and ruthlessness. The modern concept emphasizes reproductive success, which means leaving a large number of surviving progeny. Strength and sturdiness are important only insofar as they contribute to this. The "fittest" is no one more spectacular than the parent of the family with the greatest number of surviving members.

Examples will convey the idea more easily than formal definitions. There are genetic constitutions in some organisms, including man, which are known to make their carriers sterile, i.e., unable to procreate, although they may be physically quite normal and vigorous. Thus, some hybrids between species of animals, and also of plants, produce no offspring at all, despite a bodily strength and vigor equal or superior to the parents. The mule is the most widely known representative of this condition. Now, the Darwinian fitness of a mule, or of a childless couple in man, is zero, however "fit" they may be in other ways. It is for this reason that many biologists prefer to apply the term "adaptive value" rather than the classical term "fitness."

Conversely, reproductive success occasionally goes with bodily weakness and even gross infirmity. Huntington's chorea is a hereditary disease in man which appears to be due to the presence of a single dominant Mendelian gene. The afflicted persons suffer a progressive and severe degeneration of the nervous system, which leads to physical and mental incapacity and ultimately to death. However, the onset of the disease occurs at various ages, and in many instances the victims appear normal in youth and often in middle age. The result is that the victims often marry and raise large families before the disease manifests itself. Insofar as Huntington's chorea does not interfere with procreation, it does not affect genetic fitness, although it is disastrous to its victim's health. Huntington's chorea may affect biological fitness only indirectly, such as by burdening the family who are obliged to support and to care for the victim.

In general, only those events which affect the carriers of a given hereditary constitution before or during the reproductive age directly influence Darwinian fitness. This goes far to explain the origin of "the thousand natural shocks that flesh is heir to" in old age. The evolutionary development of the human species has been controlled by natural selection; this selection has favored genetic endowments which make reproductive success probable; the genotypes which make their carriers liable to those infirmities which reduce or obliterate their chance to raise a progeny have mostly failed to be perpetuated. But the ability of the body to continue to function properly after the close of the reproductive age is not controlled by selection. Under primitive conditions, life expectancy is so low that few persons reach old age; those who die young contribute little to the procreation of their group, and thus are of little importance in the biological evolution of their race and species. Haldane has even speculated that under primitive conditions the group (family, tribe) may benefit, rather than suffer, by the removal of those members who have passed the peak of their usefulness.

Perhaps the objection may be raised that the above argument proves too much; after all, natural death does not always occur immediately following the production of the last child, and in man, as well as in other animals, some individuals enjoy fair health in old age. An analogy may help us to understand the situation. A watch or another mechanism which is "guaranteed" by its manufacturer to work properly, for say a year, usually functions somewhat longer than that. It would be difficult and expensive to produce a mechanism so exact that it would operate during a specified time, no less and no more. Organic evolution faces a similar problem, and its solution is similar. The organism should be so built that it resists the wear and tear and disturbances caused by its environment without impairment of its essential functions during the period when it is most useful to the welfare of the species. But, occasionally, and under favorable conditions, it may go on functioning appreciably longer.

Cooperation

Some critics of Darwin's evolutionism urged that the theory of natural selection erred in its emphasis on struggle and competition as the basis of evolutionary success. Most interesting and original among these critics was Kropotkin, who between 1890 and 1902 published several articles and a book in which he contended that mutual aid among living beings, rather than struggle, was the evolutionary force of major importance. Having been only an amateur biologist, Kropotkin was uncritical about some of the data he cited in support of his opinions, which accordingly found little favor among professional biologists. However, other authors, particularly Allee and Ashley Montagu in recent years, have revised and modernized Kropotkin's views. This newer version proves to be quite compatible with, rather than contradictory to, the modern theory of natural selection.

Indeed, the view of "nature, red in tooth and claw," in which every living being has only the alternative of "eat or be eaten" is just as unfounded as the sentimentalist view that all is sweetness and light in unspoiled nature. An individual who is so cantankerous that he always struggles with everybody, or who lives in isolation like a hermit, is certainly not a usual phenomenon in any species. The work of modern ecologists places greater and greater emphasis on communities of individuals of similar species, and on associations of organisms of different species, as natural units.

A modicum of cooperation is indeed a necessity, especially among animals, if the species is to survive. Sexual reproduction requires that females and males cooperate at least to the extent of meeting each other and performing the acts of courtship and mating. The courtship is often elaborated to become a ritual of surprising complexity. Thus, in the bower bird (*Ptilonorhynchus*), the male builds a bower consisting of boughs with flowers of a definite color, or of other objects of a similar color, and entices the female to enter it for mating. Nonbiologists have been much impressed by the lurid stories of female spiders so fierce that they capture and eat the males who venture to approach them. It is well to remember that most males escape this fate.

Care and maintenance of the offspring often involves a very elaborate series of acts, in which parents and children cooperate. Consider, for example, the instincts which make a newborn mammal able to obtain milk from the mother's breast, and which make the mother eager to feed and to care for the infant. Any genetically induced failure of parents and children to cooperate might be disastrous for the species—or at least for the genotype responsible for the failure.

In sum, natural selection is neither egotistic nor altruistic; it is opportunistic. It perpetuates those genetic constitutions which happen to exhibit a fitness superior to others at a given time, in a given place, and in a given environment.

Genotypes which are less efficient in the production of surviving offspring become less common, and finally fail to be perpetuated. By what means the superior fitness is attained, whether by struggle or by cooperation, is immaterial in the short run. In the long run this may be important, since the relationships between organisms based on cooperation are in general more stable and enduring than relationships based on struggle and conflict. Curiously enough, this is true even of the relationship between a host and a parasite. The existence of many parasites depends upon the availability of susceptible hosts; if such a parasite kills or seriously incapacitates its host, it destroys its own means of subsistence, and those of its progeny. Hence, it is to the advantage of the parasite to become innocuous, or even useful, to its host, and at the same time to acquire the most efficient means to infect the greatest number of hosts possible. Burnet and others have argued quite cogently that parasites which cause acute and mortal infections in man are chiefly those which have had only a recent association with the human species.

Fitness and the Environment

A being may be fit to live and to produce progeny in some environments, and unfit in other environments. Darwinian fitness is a function not only of the organism itself but also of the environment, of the living conditions in which the organism is placed. A diagrammatically simple illustration of the relationship between fitness and environment can be found in the many experiments made on some lower organisms. We consider here the work of Demerec and his colleagues on the resistance of the colon bacteria (*Escherichia coli*) to the antibiotic streptomycin. Streptomycin is poisonous to normal colon bacteria; if these bacteria, commonly found in the intestinal contents of man and animals, are placed on a laboratory nutrient medium to which a sufficient concentration of streptomycin has been added, most of the bacteria are killed. But occasionally one or several cells among the many millions survive, and from them can be started new cultures of streptomycin-resistant colon bacteria, which grow quite successfully on the streptomycin-containing nutrient media.

The origin of the resistant survivors is due to a hereditary change, a mutation, which occurs in about one out of every billion cells in each cell generation. Mutations which make bacteria resistant to hithertofore harmful conditions have been observed in many bacteria. The remarkable thing about the streptomycin-resistant mutants is that most of them are not merely resistant but also streptomycin-dependent. These mutants cannot grow on nutrient media that are free of streptomycin. Here we have an environmental agent, streptomycin, which is poisonous to normal bacteria, becoming a necessity to the mutant bacteria. If a culture of both streptomycin-resistant and streptomycin-dependent bacteria is placed on a nutrient medium free of streptomycin, most of the bacteria die, except for rare mutants which are again able to grow without streptomycin. Is the "normal" genotype of the colon bacteria more, or less, fit than the genotype of the mutant which is resistant to and dependent on streptomycin? The question is evidently meaningless unless the nature of the environment in which the fitness is measured is specified. In an environment free of streptomycin, the normal bacteria grow well, and mutant ones are poisoned. In an environment containing streptomycin, the mutants are fit, while the "normals" are unfit.

A genotype which is superior to another in one environment may, then, be inferior in another environment. However, the environment of any organism is variable to a certain extent. To put it in another way, any organism meets in its lifetime not just one environment but a certain range of environments. For example, organisms which inhabit the temperate or cold climatic zones of the globe encounter the seasonal environments of summer and winter. In the tropics the inhabitants have to face rainy and dry seasons. In both climates there are seasons when food is abundant and seasons when it is scarce. Within a smaller compass, day alternates with night, and when studied in detail, it can be seen that environment does not remain constant from one moment to the next. One cannot take a bath twice in the same river, said the ancient philosopher. In order to remain alive, a living being must, then, be at least tolerably fit not in just one environment but in a certain range of environments. No matter how well adapted a race living in the temperate zone may be to summer, it cannot persist in that climate unless it is able to survive the severest winters which occur.

Adaptation to Diversity of Environments

Life has solved the problem of adaptation to the diversity of environments in countless different and ingenious ways. The work of zoologists and botanists in studying the adaptive contrivances of animals and plants has disclosed some of the most fascinating situations that biology has to offer. In the most general of terms, there exist two biological methods of becoming adjusted to a diversity of environments. One is genetic diversification. The other is the genetically controlled adaptive plasticity of the phenotype. We remember that the structure and functions of the organism, its phenotype, are, at any given moment, the result of a process of growth and development, which was brought about by a certain genetic endowment, its genotype, in a certain sequence of environments. The carriers of some genotypes are environmental specialists, and are fit to live only in a certain limited range of environments.

Other genotypes react to radically different environments by developing the kind of phenotypes that are most favorable for survival and reproduction in these environments. Both methods of adaptation have been used in the evolution of all kinds of organisms, from bacteria to man. But we hope to show that man, by means of his culture, has become adaptable to the greatest variety and range of environments. This is due, in part, to his ability to make his own environments suit his own particular biological and cultural requirements.

As shown above, the species of colon bacteria always contains (or is able to produce by mutation) either genotypes which can live on food free of streptomycin, or genotypes which require streptomycin to survive. This is adaptation by means of genetic diversification. But many bacteria contain enzymes which are necessary in order for these bacteria to metabolize certain food substances only so long as these bacteria live on the kind of nutrient media that includes these food substances. When placed on different foods, the bacteria lose the enzymes, which are now superfluous. Yet, the enzymes are reacquired when the bacteria are placed back on their old diet. The presence or absence of such an enzyme is, then, a response that the living cell makes to the presence or absence of certain substances in its environment. On the other hand, certain enzymes are present in bacteria, as far as known, no matter what the food. The ability of a bacterial strain to react to environmental changes by acquiring or by losing certain enzymes, and thus demonstrate an adaptive plasticity, is evidently determined by its hereditary constitution, its genotype, and this ability to change the phenotype may be acquired or lost by a change in the genotype.

The reaction of human skin developing a suntan is another example of phenotypic plasticity. Exposure of skin to sunlight, or rather to a part of the ultraviolet spectrum of sunlight, results in the formation of a protective dark pigment. Lack of exposure results in a gradual loss of the pigment. But the ability to acquire and to lose the pigment is determined by the genotype. Albinos always react to intense sunlight by sunburns instead of by tanning; most natives of central Africa have pigment in the skin regardless of exposure to sunlight. Many utopians, beginning with Plato, visualized an ideal human society composed of members specialized by their biological heredity to perform certain functions. One would be bred to be a carpenter or a king. Others insisted that anybody could be trained to do anything just as efficiently as anybody else. Lenin maintained that under Communism any housemaid would be able to govern the state.

Genetic diversification and plasticity of the phenotype are not mutually exclusive but are complementary methods of adaptation observed in organic evolution. The very fact of the existence in nature of at least a million animal species, plus at least a quarter of a million of plant species, is a demonstration on a grand scale of the success of genetic diversification as an adaptive device. Indeed, the basic tenet of modern evolutionism, inherited from Darwin, is that the diversity of living beings in nature is an adaptive response of living matter to the diversity of environments on our planet. Organic diversity arose in evolution because life had to continuously produce new forms able to cope with the progressively more complex and diversified environments.

"The Wisdom of the Body"

The importance of the plasticity of the phenotype is just as evident. In 1925, Walter Cannon published a remarkable book entitled *The Wisdom of the Body,* in which he discussed the phenomena of homeostasis. Homeostasis is a general name for the physiological mechanisms by which a living body responds to changes in its environment in such a way that it continues to live and function normally.

The maintenance of a constant body temperature in man and in other warm-blooded animals is an obvious example of homeostasis. This is brought about by several coordinated physiological mechanisms which keep the body temperature constant to within some tenths of a degree in the face of much greater temperature changes in the environment. Another example is the maintenance of a remarkably constant concentration of salt in the blood. If too much salt is taken in, the kidneys remove the excess via the urine; if the salt intake is low the kidneys let very little salt escape in the urine. As another example, the blood composition changes if the respiration yields only a limited supply of oxygen, as happens during a prolonged sojourn in extremely high altitudes. The changes, increasing the number of the red blood corpuscles, and so on, make a sufficient oxygen supply easier to obtain. The healing of wounds or knitting of bone fractures involves a series of processes, the remarkable correlation of which accomplishes, within limits, the repair and restoration of the injured body parts. But perhaps most remarkable of all is the formation of antibodies and antitoxins which localize or eliminate infections. Here we meet with the marvelous ability of the body to respond to the invasion of parasitic microorganisms by specific reactions which are effective against the particular kind of parasite which has provoked the reactions.

The "wisdom" of life has impressed, and often dazzled, observers from Aristotle to our day. An understanding of this wisdom in scientific terms was far from easy come by, and verbal pseudo-solutions have been invented again and again. The most persistently recurring of the pseudo-solutions is to say that this adaptiveness, this obvious and striking purposefulness of body structures and functions, is due to some inscrutable principle, for which some rather fancy names have been coined: entelechy, psyche, psychoid, vital force, perfecting principle, vital urge, or what have you. Or else, the adaptiveness of the living body to its environment has been without further ado declared an intrinsic property of living matter. This is precisely the pseudo-solution proposed for the so-called "First Law" stated by Lamarck: "By continued use, an organ in animals becomes greatly strengthened and enlarged to an extent which is proportional to the amount of its use. On the other hand, by continued disuse, an organ becomes weaker and deteriorates, finally disappearing."

But why should use strengthen an organ? It was far too difficult a problem for Lamarck to solve. The way towards a scientific explanation of the "wisdom of the body" was blazed by Darwin, but only in recent years has a more satisfactory insight into the problem become possible. As we know, heredity transmits from parents to offspring not fixed characters or traits, but rather sets the reactions of the developing organism to the environment. In other words, we have not inherited from our parents a body temperature, but rather a pattern of physiological processes which react to temperature changes in the environment by maintaining a certain temperature. We have not inherited the healing of wounds or knitting of fractured bones, but rather a pattern of reactions which are set in operation by injuries and fractures. And we do not transmit to our children antibodies to cope with every infection, but instead we give them a capacity to respond to infection by an elaboration of antibodies.

It is the genotype that determines the reactions of the organism to different environments. The fitness of the carrier of a given genotype is, then, dependent on the usefulness or harmfulness of that genotype's reactions in the environments which the carrier encounters during its life, up to the close of its reproductive age. Countless genotypes with different reaction patterns are formed in every species by mutation and sexual reproduction. Natural selection perpetuates the genotypes which react to promote survival and reproduction in the environments which the species encounters more or less regularly in the territory which it inhabits. Selection fails to perpetuate the genotypes which yield less successful phenotypes. Many genotypes react favorably in some environments but unfavorably in others; some of them are so specialized that they survive only in a narrow range of environments. The evolutionary fate of such narrow specialists will depend on the abundance of environments to which they are adapted, and on the degree of superiority which they achieve in these specialized environments.

The "wisdom of the body" is, then, not a mysterious gift or an inherent property of all life. This "wisdom" has been built slowly and painfully in the long process of evolution and is controlled by natural selection. The lack of inherent purposefulness in living things becomes strikingly apparent if an organism is placed in artificial environments or in environments which the species has seldom if ever encountered in its evolutionary history. The responses of the organism in such new environments are far from always being adaptive. Thus, tropical plants and animals transferred to our climate die of cold weather, while native ones go into winter dormancy or are otherwise able to cope with the situation. This is exactly what should be expected; the genotypes of the inhabitants of the tropics have not been selected to respond adaptively to the stimulus of cold. The human body reacts to protect itself against ultraviolet radiation of moderate intensity. It is, however, defenseless against X rays and radium rays. Man is unable to subsist on many diets which are satisfactory to some animals; for example, he cannot live long on a diet of raw grass or browse on foliage. A horse or a deer can do so. Man is not immune to certain infections to which other animals are immune. About half a century ago, Mechnikov compiled a long list of "imperfections of the human nature." Many of these imperfections concern situations which are probably too recent, in the evolutionary sense, to have been corrected by natural selection.

Constant and Variable Environments

A question now logically presents itself: If the response of a genotype in different environments is a product of evolution by natural selection, why is it that some traits appear in all environments in which life is possible, while other traits are evoked only by some special influences? Every human being has a heart with four chambers, hemoglobin in his blood, certain digestive enzymes, and a body temperature which is fairly constant except when fever is provoked by infection or by the administration of certain drugs. On the other hand, such characteristics as skin color and body weight are much more plastic, and the human disposition, at least in some people, changes from deep gloom to elation, or vice versa, within a matter of minutes.

The most enlightening approach to this problem is to consider the influence of the constancy or variability of a trait on the fitness of the organism. The constant features cited as examples in the foregoing paragraph—heart structure, regulated body temperature—are absolutely essential for the life of the human body. Accidents which affect the essential functions of the body cause death, while the gradual decline of these functions in old age results in senility and "natural" death. It is easy to see that natural selection in the evolutionary process will tend to insure that the organs and functions of the body which are necessary for life will develop in all individuals. A genotype which causes failures or abnormalities in the development of essential organs and functions for the environments which the species normally meets will fail to be perpetuated.

Schmalhausen and others have pointed out that the greater variety of environments which a species encounters, the greater will be the fitness of those genotypes which make the development of essential organs and functions autonomous and independent of environmental variations. Natural selection in favor of such genotypes is important in evolution; Schmalhausen called it "stabilizing" selection. Stabilizing selection makes the development of the organism homeostatic; and homeostatic development insures that the body will always have all the essential structures and functions it needs to survive in and reproduce in the environment which its species meets in its usual habitat.

If the hereditary endowment of all individuals were uniform and the development of all was perfectly homeostatic, then all individuals would be identical, at least those at similar ages. Such complete uniformity might be favorable for survival in an absolutely constant and unchanging world. But in the world we live in conditions vary from place to place and from time to time. Living beings must have a capacity to adapt themselves to changing conditions. In man, a dark skin is desirable in countries where the sunshine is intense throughout the year, or during the summer in those countries which have seasonably changeable climates. However, when sunshine is deficient, it is a light skin pigmentation that is deemed desirable. Accordingly, natural selection may promote either uniformity or diversity. Under variable environmental (in this case, climatic) conditions, a genetically controlled responsiveness of the organism to external influences contributes to fitness. If a darker skin color is advantageous in summer and a lighter color in winter, then a genotype which causes the development of a constant amount of pigment is less fit than one which permits the pigmentation to vary with sun exposure. Phenotypic plasticity is the only possible adaptation to changes in weather—at least in the higher organisms which live long enough to face many changes of weather.

Natural Selection In Higher and Lower Organisms

It has been pointed out above that a bacterial culture may contain a few mutant cells which are resistant to streptomycin, but which are usually also streptomycin-dependent and, then, unable to grow without this substance. These mutant cells are inviable or poorly viable in "normal" environments, i.e., in the absence of streptomycin. But they become highly useful when the environment changes by introduction of streptomycin, since then they are the only ones that survive. A bacterial culture, of course, does not "know" whether an accident, or an experimenter, will or will not expose it to streptomycin.

The mutants are produced anyhow, at a small rate of about one per every billion cells. Thus, most of them die, but their death is the price which the species pays to preserve its adaptability to a different environment.

In higher organisms, every individual is too valuable to the species to be wasted in the relatively inefficient process of adapting to environmental changes by natural selection. This sacrifice of the individual for the benefit of the species reduced more and more as the evolution of the living world progressed. Patterns of development in an individual animal appeared which possessed the property of homeostasis. The "wisdom of the body" buffered that body against the kinds of environmental disturbances which the species was likely to encounter in its normal native habitats. This permitted the life span of the individual to increase, and the fecundity of the species to which it belonged to become less, because the fewer individuals that are destroyed by environmental accidents, the fewer need to be born to maintain the species. But those individuals who do survive are masters of their environments.

Natural selection has become, however, more, rather than less, efficient as a consequence. The tremendous reproductive powers of lower organisms mean only that all but a small fraction of their progenies usually perish, and this mass destruction is in the main accidental with respect to the adaptedness of individuals of these lower organisms to their environment. Mass destruction does not promote natural selection, as is imagined by some popular writers. It rather hinders selection, because the "accident rate" of an excellent genotype is only slightly less than that of a poor one. Accidental loss of genotypes is selectively neutral or negative. Conversely, natural selection becomes most efficient and most creative when accidental loss is minimized, and when the fitness of every individual is tested thoroughly by exposure to the largest possible variety of environments.

When every individual counts in the measure of fitness, genetic specialization is too crude an adaptive instrument. As we will show, this is especially true for genetically specialized, innate or instinctive behavior. A flexibility of the development pattern, with homeostatic responses to environmental variations, is the solution. In higher animals, particularly in higher vertebrates, behavior is increasingly modifiable by learning.

At the human stage of evolution, a vastly more important refinement of adaptation to the environment has occurred. For on the animal level learning is not cumulative. Whatever experience is acquired by an individual or a generation, it is not transmitted to the next generation. The next generation has to start again from the beginning. This is indeed not surprising; there is no biological mechanism that can transmit acquired characters. Among animals, evolutionary improvements, including improvements of behavior, still have to take place by the rigid and slow method of transmission of genes from parents to progeny, immediate or remote, but to nobody else. This method of evolution is simply unable to keep up with the speed and efficiency of action that is requisite because of the complexity of human environments and their rapid changes.

Man is the only biological species which managed to free itself in part from this limitation of biological heredity. He did so by evolving the transmission of culture, which is a new, nonbiological heredity. Every individual in every generation still must learn for himself what the experience of the past generations has to teach him, but the learning can be telescoped into a fraction of the mean lifetime. The important thing is that the learning acquired may then be passed on to anybody, above and beyond the limitations imposed by the biological mechanism of gene transfer.

Does Natural Selection Continue to Operate in Modern Man?

The genetic endowment of mankind has been forged in the process of an evolution controlled by natural selection. But does natural selection still operate in man? The assertion often met with, especially in popular writings on the biology of man, is that it does not. Our living conditions are, allegedly, so "unnatural" that natural selection has ceased to operate in human societies, especially in the technologically advanced ones. Man lives too well protected from inclement weather by his clothing and housing; he is too well fed; he has grown "soft" since he no longer needs to struggle with wild beasts and only rarely engages in hand-to-hand fighting with his human enemies. Most important of all, medicine is saving the lives of many weaklings who would surely die off under the conditions in which the man of the Old Stone Age and even the savages of today are forced to live. Now these weaklings not only stay alive but beget families. Another insidious influence is that the more well-to-do classes in the population produce fewer children per family than do the lower classes. Since the economic status is supposedly correlated positively with native intelligence, this differential fertility leads to an unnatural selection in favor of lower intelligence. According to Cook, the average intelligence of the population of the United States should be declining at the rate of from two to four I.Q. points per generation. Pretty soon "there will not be enough competent people to keep the wheels of industry, commerce, and government on the rails."

No detailed discussion of these complex and controversial issues can be attempted in this short work. It is not out of place, however, to consider some basic premises on which such a discussion should be based. To begin with, much confusion arises from misusing the word "natural." If one considers as "natural" only the selection which was taking place in the environment of cave men, then obviously there can be no natural selection in any other environments. But such a restriction is unwarranted. Selection occurs in any environment in which the carriers of different genotypes do not transmit their genes to the progeny at equal rates. To do away with selection in man, all kinds of people would have to produce the same average numbers of surviving children. This is not the case now, and well may one doubt that such a situation will ever be reached.

Natural selection is distinguished from artificial selection. The latter occurs when the contributions of various genetic types to the hereditary endowment of the next generation are decided not by the environment but by a human authority. It is man who decides which bulls are used for breeding and which are to be castrated or killed for meat. In man, artificial selection would mean that the number of children which every couple produced would be regulated by some eugenic authority, or else decided by the prospective parents themselves. This is the ideal of classical eugenics, which is far from having been realized. Natural selection is going on in all human societies, nonliterate as well as literate ones. What has happened repeatedly, and what will doubtless continue to happen, is that the selection varies in direction and in intensity at different times and in different places.

It is the environment which decides whether the streptomycin-resistant or the streptomycin-sensitive colon bacteria survive or are wiped out. The characteristics which were favored by natural selection in man of the Old Stone Age are not the same as those favored in man of the Iron Age, and these may not be favored in man of the Atomic Age. Selection favors what is useful in the existing environment, not what was useful in the past or what will be useful at some future date. Man lives in environments created by his culture and his technology, and these environments determine what selection is doing. With steam heat and adequate clothing, we do not need to be adapted to the way of life of the old Fuegians, who could resist freezing weather with little clothing on. With the food supply assured, the ability to stand periodic starvation becomes of little import. In fact, some people now have to cope with a danger rarely met with before— the danger of systematic overeating. With our police doing their duty, the ability to win in a brawl with fisticuffs is less important than the ability to live in harmony with one's neighbors.

It is obvious that health, appearance, conformity to the standards of behavior accepted in a given society or social stratum, and the willingness and ability to have, bring up, and provide for children, now influence and always have influenced the number of genes which a human individual transmits to the gene pool of the succeeding generation. It is likely that some or all of these variables are conditioned in part by the nature of the genotype of the person involved, and that the conditioning may be different in different environments. This goes far to insure that genetic selective processes operate in human societies, advanced as well as primitive.

As to intelligence, there is no conclusive evidence to show whether the trend in recent times has been towards a lowering of the intelligence level, as Cook and other alarmists contend. The only pertinent study, in which the I.Q. level of the schoolchildren in Scotland was measured twice a little less than a generation apart, has indicated, if anything, that the level has risen slightly. But, for argument's sake, let us suppose that the families which produce fewer children in our society are genetically better endowed with respect to intelligence than are, on the average, the families with many children. If so, the genetic basis of intelligence would be expected to become weakened. But this would not mean that natural selection ceased to operate; selection favors higher Darwinian fitness, and the fitness of a genotype is measured and judged by its reproductive success. Intelligence may increase fitness, or it may lower it. But if, in a given society, one must be not-too-bright in order to have many children, then, a lower intelligence increases the fitness of a genotype and a higher intelligence lowers it. This may seem a paradox. Actually it means only that natural selection does not necessarily favor what *we* may regard as desirable.

The Limitations of Natural Selection

It has been pointed out above that natural selection is opportunistic. It always favors those genetic endowments which yield maximum reproductive success in a given environment. But what is favorable today may not be so tomorrow. It is a fallacy to think that mankind would be safe if only natural selection were permitted to operate. It does operate, but this is no guarantee of biological safety. The geological strata of the earth's crust contain fossilized remains of countless thousands of species which became extinct without issue. Yet the evolution of these species was controlled by natural selection. They became extinct mostly because natural selection made them too specialized to live in environments which were only temporary.

Man has acquired an intelligence which makes him audacious enough to question whether natural selection steers the evolution in the direction which he considers good and desirable. In the near future man probably will have learned enough to influence the direction of the evolutionary changes in his own species by introducing well-considered and agreed-upon pressures of artificial selection. The chief difficulty may then be not the method of accomplishing a given plan, but the agreement to choose a plan to be accomplished. There is no conclusive evidence to show whether the selective trend in recent times has been towards a lowering of the intelligence level or not. If it has, it has assumed this pernicious direction only in some human populations, and in these only in recent times. Countermeasures may have to be taken, and it is perhaps not unduly optimistic to hope that an improved understanding of human biology and a greater diffusion of biological knowledge may make such a plan for steering his own evolution realizable in practice.

Human and Animal Societies

Are we morally free beings, or wheels in a machine? I prefer to think of life, and consequently of history, as a goal achieved, and not as means to something else. ALEXANDER HERZEN

The Lord of Creation

Judged by any reasonable criteria, man represents the highest, most progressive, and most successful product of organic evolution. The really strange thing is that so obvious an appraisal has been over and over again challenged by some biologists. Suppose, it has been argued, that evolution is studied not by man but by a fish. Would not the highest form of animal then have to be a fish? To which Simpson has replied: "I suspect that the fish's reaction would be, instead, to marvel that there are men who question that man is the highest animal. It is not beside the point to add that the 'fish' that made such judgments would have to be a man!"

The evidence of the success of man as a biological species is ample and overwhelming. No one can tell how numerous was the prehuman species from which man has evolved, but it is certain that the human population has increased greatly following the invention of agriculture. The world population at the time of the Roman Empire is estimated to have been some 150 to 200 millions; around A.D. 1650 it was between 500 and 550 millions. The estimate for 1947 is about 2,330 millions. The increase in number is, of course, not the only form of biological success, and it may be a disaster if it leads to uncontrolled overpopulation. However, man has become one of the few truly cosmopolitan species. He has penetrated into all parts of the earth's surface, and has established permanent habitation on all continents and major islands, except in Antarctica (and even there he manages to live for short periods of time). He has, accordingly, become exposed to every variety of geographic environment which the world has to offer, and he has become adapted to these environments. But, while animals and plants become adapted to their environments by modifying their bodies and their genes, man has remained the same and has to a considerable extent modified environments to suit his purposes and his preferences, and has created completely new environments.

Furthermore, man has himself become an evolutionary agent. He has been able to destroy many species of animals and plants, some of them deliberately and many thoughtlessly. He has learned to control, and in some cases to eradicate, other species which had preyed on him or on the products of his labors as parasites or pests. He became able to modify the biological evolution of those species which he domesticated in a direction which suited his interests or fancies. Most remarkable of all, he is now in the process of acquiring knowledge which may permit him, if he so chooses, to control his own evolution. He may yet become "business manager for the cosmic process of evolution," a role which Julian Huxley has ascribed to him, perhaps prematurely.

Man is a social animal who lives in organized groups with other men, and who cannot live otherwise for more than a generation—and rarely that long. Man is also the biological species which possesses the capacity to create and to transmit to succeeding generations "the social legacy the individual acquires from his group," i.e., the ability to create and to transmit culture. He is the only species which has developed culture, and the emergence of such a species has been a unique event in the history of all life on this earth, and perhaps also in the history of the Cosmos. He is, however, by no means the only social animal, and his society is by no means the only one known among animals. Being a social animal does not mean that one is necessarily a cultural animal, although the development of the capacity to have a culture is possible presumably only in a social animal. The genetic basis of culture is, then, different from that of social habits, and so is the adaptive function of culture different from that of society. A comparison of human and animal societies may throw light on the nature of both.

Highly Organized Insect Societies

Allee has characterized societies as "all groupings of individuals which are sufficiently integrated so that natural selection can act on them as units." If the degree of integration is taken as a measure of the perfection of a society, then the most advanced social organizations are unquestionably found among social insects, and particularly among ants and termites. Here, the division of labor is carried to the point where biologically the most important function of any organism, i.e., procreation, is borne by a specialized caste, while most of the other individuals who compose the society remain sexually undeveloped. In some termite and ant nests, containing thousands or tens of thousands of individuals, there may exist only a single fertile female. A "queen" in some termite species may lay several thousand eggs in every twenty-four hours, and may continue doing so without interruption for several years. Her abdomen is so distended by enormous ovaries that she can neither procure food nor move by herself. She is, in effect, a living egg factory, immured in a special cell in the interior of the nest, and conscientiously and continuously tended by numerous workers. In the honeybee and in some ants, the queen mates with a male only once in her lifetime, during the mating flight which usually precedes the foundation of the colony.

In addition to one or more "queens" and males, an ant or termite colony may contain numerous individuals belonging to "worker" castes. In some species, all workers carry on different functions as the occasion requires. In others, there is a worker caste proper, which takes care of procuring food and building the nest and keeping it in good repair. A soldier caste defends the colony from intruders. A curious caste are the "repletes" in honey ants, the function of whom is to serve as storage barrels for food (stowed away in their inflated bellies). Among other curiosities in ants are individuals with "phragmotic" heads, which fit like plugs into the entrance holes leading into the nest. These individuals function as "doormen," since they withdraw and permit the passage of individuals of their own colony, but not of outsiders.

It is well established by suitable experiments that members of an ant or a termite colony recognize each other and differentiate between nest-mates and strangers. Among ants, not only the nest itself but also a certain amount of the surrounding territory is defended against all comers. The owners of the territory frequently fight and may kill the intruders, including individuals from other nests of the same species. It appears that, at least in some ants, the sense used to discriminate between nest-mates and outsiders is that of smell. Every member of a colony seems to share one common family odor, and any individual who does not have that odor is treated as an enemy. Conversely, every member of a colony shows a complete "devotion" to the commonwealth. Readiness to sacrifice life itself is certainly the supreme test of the devotion an individual feels for another individual or for the community, and members of an insect society are often subjected to this trial. Members of the soldier caste, where such is present, or the undifferentiated workers in species which have no soldiers, attack the enemy, even one vastly stronger than themselves, completely heedless of danger. The sting of a honeybee worker has reversed barbs, and is often left in the flesh of her victim; the bee who loses her sting is, however, mortally wounded in the process, and it dies soon thereafter. A bee attacking an enemy with her sting is thus committing suicide.

Many insects perform wonderfully complex, coordinated operations which, in the environments where the species normally lives, promote the survival and reproduction of the individual or benefit its progeny. Among social insects, members of a colony may carry out intricate cooperative undertakings which aid the commonwealth. Thus, some species of termites and ants build nests of a kind of elaborate architecture that is strictly characteristic of their own species and is different in different species. The sauva ants (*Atta*) feed chiefly on special fungi which they cultivate in their nests. Probably everybody who has had a chance to observe life in the forests of tropical America has seen long files of sauva workers carrying to their subterranean nests portions of leaves which they had cut from a large variety of plants. In the nest, other workers chew the leaves to a spongy pulp which is stored in special chambers and infected with spores of a fungus. The mycelial growth and the fruiting bodies of the fungus are then used to feed all members of the colony. It is interesting to note that the sexually developed individuals which establish new colonies transport a pellet of the fungus with them, and feed the first crop of new workers on fungi grown on their own excrements. When the workers appear, they immediately take to leaf cutting and to the construction of fungus "gardens" for the new nest.

Perhaps no other feature of the biology of ants has impressed observers as much as the ability of certain species to wage organized warfare against other species, and to secure for themselves and to profit by the work of "slaves." From time to time the workers of the ant *Polyergus* form raiding parties which surge from their own nest to invade that of another species of ants in the neighborhood. The raiders overwhelm the resistance of the owners, kill many of the defenders, enter the nest, seize the larvae and pupae of the victims, and carry them off to their own nest. Curiously enough, the adult workers which hatch from these larvae and pupae become faithful "slaves" who serve their captors as they would their own colonies. Some slave-making species of ants are unable to secure their own food and to maintain their own nests, and are entirely dependent on slave labor for their existence.

Anthropomorphic Fallacies

It was to be expected that some scientists were overly inspired by these observations of social insects, and were so carried away by their enthusiasm as to suggest that man may well learn from insect societies how to organize or improve his own societies. Surely, there is little to admire in slavery and in slave raids, but, on the other hand, the absolute and selfless "devotion" of an individual bee, ant, or termite to the common weal of the colony are admirable. They seem to show a high degree of integrity and heroism which we rightly admire in some of our fellow men. The whole life of these insects appears to display unflinching purposefulness, which all too often we seek in vain in humans.

It is really unfortunate that a closer scrutiny makes the

whole pretty picture disappear like a dream. Finding al-
truism and other human qualities in insects proves to be
a delusion. Ants and termites are neither heroes when
they defend their own nests, nor villains when they rob
those of their neighbors. They are devoid of virtues and
vices because they lack the freedom to decide between
possible alternative courses of action. They act as they do
because their behavior represents an innate response to
a given environmental situation. Insect behavior is, then,
not reducible to a common ethical measure with human
actions. Praise and blame have meaning only in connection with acts in which the individual is at least to some
extent a free agent. Although they show some interesting
parallels, human societies and insect societies are distinct
phenomena.

The insect is born fully equipped to perform the often
very complex work by means of which its species secures
its livelihood and provides for its offspring. A larva of a
caddis fly just hatched from its egg proceeds to build its
house in a characteristic way and from certain materials
although it has never seen another larva building a house.
An ant is ready to participate in the activities of its nest-
mates soon after it hatches from its pupa. It does not
undergo a period of training or apprenticeship.

This does not mean that the insect is an automaton able
to do just one thing. Far from this. A bee worker hatched
from the pupa spends her first two or three days incubating
the brood and preparing brood cells. Then follow about
three days during which the worker feeds the older larvae
with honey and pollen, and four to nine days in which

she feeds the younger larvae with brood food. A two-weeks-old bee now takes her first trial flight outside the hive, and for the next ten days or so she works as a "house bee," receiving and storing the food brought by other bees, cleaning the hive, and guarding its entrance. Only after that period does she become a field worker, foraging for pollen and nectar. There is even conclusive evidence to show that insects are capable of some simple learning—such as associating the presence of food with marks of certain colors and shapes. But, as Haskins puts it: "It is as though the invertebrate mind functioned like a shallow vessel which, once filled, cannot be emptied. By contrast, the vertebrate mind is a deeper pitcher. It may be partially emptied many times, and as often refilled with liquids of another dye. As the mammalian mind grows older, it grows wiser. Faced with a rapidly changing environment, the invertebrate mind merely grows less well adapted and more thoroughly confused."

Adaptive Advantages of Innate and Learned Behavior

The great advantages and the equally considerable limitations of innate, or instinctive, behavior are obvious. Every individual of a species (except rare and pathological deviants) is born adapted to the environment which he is likely to encounter. An individual needs no training or preparation for the business of living. He is born fully prepared by his genotype. And the genotype is, in turn, molded in the evolutionary process and controlled by natural selection. As shown earlier, the adaptation to the environment by means of genotypic specialization is advantageous in a relatively constant environment. The "wisdom" of instinct is a distillation of the experience of the species in the environments which it has met regularly, or at least repeatedly, during its evolution. The adaptation reached by a genotypic fixation of behavior may be extremely precise and subtle. The individual does exactly what is best for himself and for his species. He does exactly what he should do at precisely the right time.

The drawback of genotypic specialization and fixation is that the possibilities of adaptation to environmental changes become severely limited. Numerous and ingenious experiments have shown that when an animal is placed in novel environments, its innate behavior loses its "wisdom." The animal is likely to do exactly the wrong thing, damaging its own chance of survival or that of its offspring. A commonplace example of such grossly unadaptive behavior is the attraction of many species of insects to light, resulting in their death in countless numbers near electric and other lighting fixtures. More refined experiments regarding instincts have been made by Fabre, on many insects, and by Lorenz and Tinbergen, chiefly on vertebrates. They agree in showing that innate behavior tends to be fixed, predictable, uniform, and adaptive under normal living conditions. But this behavior shows relatively little capacity for adaptive modification when confronted with unusual circumstances.

Conversely, the capacity to learn causes the animal to modify its behavior in accordance with the circumstances of its individual life experience. Learned behavior is not separate from or independent of innate behavior; it is, rather, a modification of the latter. Tinbergen defines learning as "a central nervous process causing more or less lasting changes in the innate behavioral mechanisms under the influence of the outer world." Some capacity to learn is present in most animals, but the relative importance of learned behavior is greater in higher than in lower animals. Expressed in genetic terms, an individual's capacity to learn permits this individual to modify his behavioral phenotype. The adaptive significance of learning ability is that it brings about a plasticity of this phenotype. The behavior is no longer determined by the animal's inherited nature within fairly narrow limits; it is also determined by the experience of living.

Innate and learned elements of behavior may be very intimately associated. According to Lorenz, the ability of jackdaws (birds belonging to the crow family) to recognize their enemies is not inborn but learned. The young birds, or birds raised in captivity, have no fear of predators who may be dangerous to them. But an old jackdaw gives a characteristic "rattling" cry when a potential enemy appears in sight. The young birds rapidly form a mental picture associating the warning "rattle" with the appearance of the enemy, and thus come to recognize this enemy. The "rattle" response is innate, as the ability so to respond is evidently conditioned by the genotype of the bird. But this innate response may become the basis of a learned behavior conditioned by a social situation.

Furthermore, jackdaws, wild or tame, will attack any

animal, including man, if the latter picks up and holds another jackdaw. In fact, it doesn't even have to be a jackdaw. Any living being that carries a black object dangling and fluttering in his hands or his mouth is treated as an enemy and provokes an attack. This behavior can be elicited even in tame jackdaws, who do not mind being picked up in human hands themselves. Here again the results of learning are superimposed on innate behavior. Once the attack response is given to an individual who has acted as an enemy, the bird tends thereafter to treat that individual as an enemy. Lorenz supposes that crows have similar sets of innate and learned responses. A man who has only once or twice been seen with a dead crow in his hands is recognized long afterwards as an enemy by the crows in the neighborhood.

What part of behavior will be innate and what will be learned is determined by the evolutionary history of the species. It is naive to think that behavioral differences between human races must be genotypic because such differences between varieties of domestic animals are largely so. Although, from the master's viewpoint, it is advantageous for him to have his animals individually trainable to some extent, the basic fact is that every variety has been bred for a specific use or purpose. Now, the psychic characteristics of a breed are evidently important for its use. A race horse with the temperament of a draft horse would hardly win many races, and a draft horse with the temperament of a race horse would have to be disposed of for the value of his hide. These breeds differ in temperament because the difference has been built into them by strict artificial selection. The breeds are genotypically specialized because otherwise they would not be as useful as they are to their masters. A laboratory mouse can be picked up by its tail, and will not make serious attempts to escape. A wild mouse, even one born in a laboratory cage, has to be handled with care if it is not to get away. Why is there such a difference in behavior? Clearly because laboratory mice are descended from those of their progenitors who did not escape.

Rudiments of the Capacity to Develop Culture

Learned behavior may be expected to be, and actually is, more important in vertebrate animals, with their highly developed brains, than among lower animals with simpler nervous systems. The brain of a fly, or even of an ant, is too imperfect an instrument to enable its possessor to learn much from experience. Moreover, an insect lives generally a relatively short time, and it must be able during that time to accomplish all that is necessary to beget progeny. It cannot afford to spend much time on training and teaching. Its behavior is genetically fixed to a large extent, and, thanks to this, the insect proceeds without delay to do the work which has to be done at its age and development stage. The work is done from the start as competently as it will ever be done; an insect learns but little by apprenticeship.

Progressive development of the cerebral cortex, together

with the lengthening of the individual life span, gave rise to a different situation in higher vertebrate animals. There, an individual does profit by experience. He can become adjusted not only to the average environment in which his ancestors used to live for many generations, but also to those which he meets in his own life. A further advance was made in human evolution. Man alone has the genes and the brain which enable him to acquire learning and to transmit it from generation to generation.

Man shares his biological pinnacle with no other species. Men learn from previous generations, and add to this learning the new knowledge which they have acquired; this is cumulative learning. Every generation stands on the shoulders of its predecessor. This difference between man and animal is fundamentally a difference in degree, but it is so great that it may justly be described as qualitative. It becomes important, then, for an evolutionist to show that some animals do have a very rudimentary capacity for cumulative learning. However minute that capacity may be, it shows that natural selection may have found in the ancestors of our species the genetic raw materials from which human intelligence was eventually constructed.

Let us consider again the observations of Lorenz on the jackdaw. Young jackdaws learn to identify potential enemies because the old ones utter the "rattling" cry when an enemy appears in sight. But the "rattling" reaction is formed originally by the visual impression of the enemy carrying a fluttering jackdaw in his clutches. It is not clear whether the identification of a species of animal as an enemy can persist for more than a single generation of jackdaws after that enemy (or an individual like it) has been seen assaulting a jackdaw. If it can so persist, it would follow that a process of transmission of acquired learning is involved. A jackdaw may transmit its fears to its offspring; but whether the offspring would in turn transmit them to the next generation without a renewal of the stimulus is uncertain.

Such a possibility is, however, open whenever the behavior of individuals is shaped to any considerable extent by training given by their parents or by other members of their species. Situations of this sort are known in higher vertebrates, and especially among birds (they may occur also in mammals, but the life of birds has been studied more extensively in nature). The kea parrot (*Nestor notabilis*) is a common bird in the mountains of the South Island of New Zealand. Its usual food consists of insect larvae, roots, berries, and seeds of various plants. In 1867 and 1868 the keas were first observed to attack and to wound sheep. Very soon keas became a menace to sheep raising in the high country of New Zealand. They developed a method of overcoming and killing live sheep, and of feeding on their flesh. The bird would jump on the sheep's back and strike with its powerful beak. The sheep attempted to get rid of the assailant, and usually rushed about madly, the bird clinging to the sheep's wool. The animal eventually fell down from exhaustion and loss of blood, and was fed upon by the keas.

Although before the arrival of man the keas had fed on very diversified diets, they could not have developed this technique of sheep killing much before 1867, since before the introduction of sheep by man, New Zealand had no other mammal of similar size. It appears that even at present sheep killing is practiced by not all but only by some individuals of keas. An even more peculiar habit has developed in tits (*Parus coeruleus* and *Parus major*) and certain other birds in the British Isles and the adjacent portion of the European continent. The first known record of tits opening the cardboard tops of milk bottles and drinking milk was made in 1921 near Southampton, in southern England. Since then, the habit of opening milk bottles spread rapidly and increased in frequency among tits with each passing year. Fisher and Hinde consider it most probable that the practice of opening milk bottles originated with relatively few individual birds. Other birds have learned from these pioneers. A possible basis which may have made the "discovery" possible is the habit which tits have of tearing bark from the twigs of the trees where they search for food. They are also known to enter human houses and to tear paper from the walls. This paper-tearing habit, applied accidentally to the paper tops of milk bottles, might have led to the reward of finding food, and might have spread to other individuals by imitation.

Rudiments of Language

Since human cultural development is intimately connected with the ability to use symbols in general and symbolic language in particular, it is interesting to find that some beginnings of such an ability are also present among animals. Curiously enough, the clearest known case is not found among apes, or even among mammals, but among insects. The remarkable experiments of Von Frisch have established that a honeybee who has found a new source of nectar is able to communicate information about its location to her hive-mates. The bee returns to the hive and performs a special symbolic "dance" which indicates the direction as well as the approximate distance from hive to food. The distance is indicated in the "dance" by a series of circles or of figures-of-eight. The direction is shown by the angles which the dancing movements take with respect to the vertical (the direction of gravity). Kroeber's analysis of the data gathered by Von Frisch shows that bee "dances" convey the information by means of symbolic acts. This seems to be definitely a symbolic language, and not a communication by means of signs or signals. The latter is common among animals, while the former is quite characteristically human.

The patient observational and experimental work of Köhler, Yerkes, Nissen, and others has disclosed that the chimpanzee is much superior to other nonhuman primates in memory, imagination, and learning ability. Nevertheless, there is a vast gulf between the intellectual capacity of chimpanzees and of man. Symbolic responses can be learned by chimpanzees only with considerable difficulty, and their frequency fails to increase with experience and age. Yerkes sums up his conclusions as follows: "By comparison with human exhibits, those taken from the life of this ape seem insignificant. Nevertheless, however re-

stricted their usefulness and however primitive and in-
stable, these exhibits merit the attention of those who
are concerned with origins and the processes of phylo-
genesis. It is even possible that except for the evolution
of anthropoid language, social tradition, and culture, almost unrecognizable though they may be as such, there
would be no human culture."

The Evolution of the Human Brain

Man's body differs so clearly from that of any other
animal that the evolutionary process which culminated
in his appearance must have involved appreciable changes
compared to the body structure of man's ancestors. Without attempting to describe these changes even briefly, it
may be stated that the two most striking innovations have
been the acquisition of an upright body posture, and,
even more specially, the remarkable development of the
brain, particularly of the cerebral cortex. One of the consequences of the upright posture has been as already
pointed out—the development of the hands and of their
ability to execute delicate operations. The advancement
of the brain has been still more spectacular.

The brain of a gorilla measures at most 650 cc. in volume, compared to a range of from slightly less than
1,000 cc. to more than 2,000 cc. for modern man. Since
the gorilla has a body weight considerably greater than
man's, the disproportion of the relative sizes is more striking than that of the volumes. The South African ape men
(*Australopithecinae*) had brains of between 415 and 650

cc. in volume, and a body weight less than that in man. The Java men (*Homo erectus*) had a brain volume of about 870 cc. Regardless of whether the South African ape men are the direct ancestors of our own species or not, it is clear that a tremendous expansion of the absolute as well as of the relative size of the brain has taken place during human evolution. Numerous changes in the skull became necessary to accommodate the expanding brain. Indirectly these changes involved the entire body.

Many alterations in the body, which when considered in isolation do not seem to have any apparent usefulness, are subservient to the main trend of human evolution—the development of the brain and its functions. In the words of Weidenreich: "One of the most impressive experiences a student of human evolution can have is to realize the extent to which all the smaller structural alterations of the human skull are correlated with and dependent upon each other and the extent to which they are governed by the trend of the skull transformation as a whole. These details, which are scarcely recognizable when only the usual anthropological methods of measurement are applied and which have been badly neglected in the past, give clear evidence of the continuity of human evolution through all known phases."

The leading role of the expansion of the brain in human phyletic evolution is understandable. The fitness of an organism is, it should be remembered, a result of the summation of its favorable and unfavorable reactions to its environment. Man is neither particularly strong in body nor particularly agile in movement. If it were not for his brain he would be a rather pitiable misfit in most environments, and would probably have become extinct long before now. It is his capacity to acquire and to accumulate experience and knowledge that made him an unprecedented biological success.

It may be asked whether the capacity to learn and to handle symbols developed as a result of the superior development of the brain, or vice versa. This question belongs in the same class as the puzzle of which came first— the chicken or the egg. It is clear that, to have acquired even the rudiments of a transmissible culture, considerable development of the cerebral cortex was necessary. Our ancestors were becoming more and more intelligent animals, and this fact gave them a high fitness. Now, the increase of fitness owing to the ability to transmit the experience gained from one generation to another placed greater and greater adaptive value on further development of the brain. The two processes, growth of the brain's capacity to assimilate culture and growth of the culture, must have been interconnected throughout human evolution. They continue to be interdependent at present.

This contradicts the fairly widespread notion that whatever natural selection could have done in developing the intellectual abilities of man, it had finished by the time the human stage of evolution was reached. It has, for example, been stated that there is no evidence of any change in human intellectual capacities since the times when masterly paintings were executed on the walls of caves during the Aurignacian period. At least one writer has gone so far as to doubt whether modern man is intellectually appreciably more able than the Java man was.

Studies of nonliterate societies disclose that in such

societies almost every sexually mature and healthy individual eventually succeeds in obtaining a chance for mating. Some writers concluded from this that selection, and particularly selection for higher intelligence, did not operate in primitive peoples. Clearly, such a conclusion is not an inevitable one. To begin with, the number of children produced is a function of the frequency of mating, which is rarely, if ever, uniform for all members of a population. Even more to the point is the fact that the ability to bring up children successfully depends to a considerable extent on the position of the parents in the community. The enormous literature on primitive and advanced cultures accumulated by anthropologists and ethnographers has apparently never been examined with the viewpoint of studying the opportunities that these cultures offer for natural selection to operate as a determinant of higher intelligence. However, it is obvious, from even a superficial acquaintance with this literature, that different societies are not equivalent in this respect. Most likely, natural selection has always operated, although with varying intensities, in the direction of the maintenance and growth of intelligence and educability.

Man as an Evolutionary Novelty

No one can tell just when the human phase of evolution started or how long its different stages took. The critical step from animal to man might have taken some hundreds of thousands of years, which is very rapid for an evolutionary change of so great a magnitude. According to Coon, our remote ancestors might have used unworked flint tools as early as in late Pliocene times, a million or more years ago. The South African man ape (*Australopithecus prometheus*) was thought by its discoverer to have used fire, but this is not regarded as certain by others, and anyway the dating of this find is uncertain. The oldest undoubted evidence of the use of fire is associated with the Peking man (*Homo erectus pekinensis*), who lived perhaps 300,000 years ago or less. By about 35,000 years ago, again according to Coon, man learned to cook food and to sew cloth. About 6,000 years ago he invented agriculture, and about 5,000 years ago, writing.

The evolution of man represents one of the rare instances of the emergence, in the history of life, of a radically new kind of biological organization, and of the adoption of an entirely novel way of life. Such evolutionary "discoveries" occur usually by rapid transitions, described by Simpson as "quantum" evolution. Quantum evolution may lead to the formation of new, higher, biological categories, such as new orders or classes. But, as pointed out by Simpson, it may give rise only to new species or genera. The important thing is that the new group adopts a way of life completely distinct from its ancestors. Mankind remains a vertebrate, a mammal, a primate, and it shares the suborder *Anthropoidea* with monkeys and apes. But man is the sole living representative of a family *Hominidae*, which most authorities regard as distinct from the nearest related family, *Pongidae*, to which belong the apes.

To say that man arose by quantum evolution does **not**

mean, of course, that he arose overnight, by some sort of "systemic mutation" as is imagined by some biologists. There is no evidence at all that systemic mutations have occurred in the evolution of man or in that of any other group of organisms. Quantum evolution is rapid only in terms of geological time-scales. What is important is not so much the speed of the process but the fact that it involved a pronounced break in the biological continuity. Man's body acquired some novel adaptations, such as the freeing of the anterior extremities from the walking duties. The basic novelty was, however, the development of unprecedented intellectual abilities, which made possible the control of the environment by the novel method of culture. The appearance of man inaugurated a third kind of history, the history of culture, superimposed upon cosmic and upon biological evolutionary histories.

Necessity and Freedom

I am among those who think well of the human character generally. I consider man as formed for society, and endowed by nature with those dispositions which fit him for society. I believe also . . . that his mind is perfectible to a degree of which we cannot as yet form any conception.

THOMAS JEFFERSON

Nothing But an Animal?

Discovery is an exciting business. But when one discovers a new truth, or hears of new truth discovered by others, there is likely to arise a temptation. This is the temptation to think that the new truth explains everything, instead of only something, in the world. Scientists, because of their occupation, may be privileged to feel the joy of discovery more often; they are also more likely to fall prey to the temptation. Biologists have learned much about living beings; they begin to have a glimmer of understanding about how living beings operate. Man is a living being; he is a part of nature; what can be more natural than to suppose that he operates as do other living beings? And so he does, in many important ways. But in some ways he is unique, and it is just as wrong to explain human affairs entirely by biology as to suppose that biology has no bearing on human affairs.

Species and breeds of animals often differ in behavior, temperament, and capacity to be trained for different uses. This is particularly true of domestic animals. Compare the nervous, high-strung, and impetuous race horse with the placid, powerful, and reliable draft horse. Or compare a turbulent fox terrier with a sedate St. Bernard. These differences are to a considerable degree genetic, although horses and dogs of all breeds can be trained to perform different kinds of work. But is the same thing true of different breeds of men? To Lush, an outstanding American animal breeder, this seems obvious: "To anyone familiar with animals it is well-nigh impossible to understand the reluctance of some psychologists to study or even to admit the role of heredity in innate mental differences between individuals in the same family and strain. Even our grandfathers knew well that such things played a large part in animal behavior and that many of these mental differences were hereditary in the sense that they 'ran in families' more than could possibly be explained as caused entirely by cultural transfer. What possible reasons can there be for our reluctance to accept the same conclusions for man or even to study it in human beings, except that we feel instinctively that some of the consequences would be personally repugnant to us?"

There is every reason, indeed, to study humans as well as animals, but not to ascribe hastily to man anything or everything that we find in animals. In the first place, man is a social animal, and the evolution of psychic traits in social animals may differ in some respects from that in solitary or in socially weak forms. Moreover, man is the only existing "political" animal, and he is involved not in one but in two evolutions. He evolves biologically, as do other organisms. But he evolves also culturally, and cultural evolution is uniquely human. This uniquely human evolution is based on a principle which is almost completely foreign to the nonhuman world—the transmission of acquired knowledge from one generation to another. Attempts to treat man as though he were "nothing but an animal" are naive and ingenuous. Man is man, as well as animal. The differences between the evolutionary patterns in the human species and those in other organisms we shall now consider.

Evolutionary Diversification or Unity

Viewed in the perspective of time, two main types of evolutionary changes may be distinguished. The changes may be cumulative and may lead in the same general direction, making the descendants more and more unlike their ancestors as the time sequence progresses. Such changes are called "phyletic" evolution by Simpson, and "anagenetic" by Rensch. Anagenesis, or phylesis, gives rise to new forms of life, without, however, increasing the diversity of organisms—species still remains a single species, although it changes its appearance. On the other hand, a species may become split into two or more races, and these may diverge and become derived species. As a result, two or more species are found where only one existed before. The diversity of life has become increased. This is called "splitting" by Simpson, and "cladogenesis" by Rensch.

The evolution of the human stock has involved both anagenesis and cladogenesis, but with a distinct predominance of the former. Weidenreich was apparently the first to point out the remarkable fact that, as far as paleontological data go, there is no evidence that more than a single human or subhuman species ever existed at any one time level. Although some recent findings of subhuman remains in South Africa may require this conclusion to be revised, it will still be true that mankind has preserved its biological unity with extraordinary tenacity.

The human species may never have split into several species coexistent on the same time level, but processes of splitting (cladogenesis) and evolutionary diversification nevertheless did occur in human evolution. Mankind became differentiated into races.

This could hardly have been otherwise when man spread throughout the world, from subpolar regions to the equator, and encountered a vast variety of climatic and biological environments. A species becomes differentiated into races in response to the environmental conditions which prevail in the territories which these races occupy. Each race possesses a high fitness in its own territory, but not necessarily in territories in which other races live. Race divergence may progress to the point where the unity of the species is lost, and two or several incipient, derived species are present instead.

However, there is nothing inevitable about racial divergence. Races do not necessarily become species. The process can also be reversed, and races may converge and fuse into a single population if intermarriage between their representatives becomes frequent. Races can either become more different or more similar. It is all a matter of whether the genetic forces leading to divergence, or whether those tending towards convergence, get the upper hand. Divergence is promoted by those environmental differences which cause natural selection to favor different genotypes in different geographic regions. With man, cultural developments have served to equalize, rather than to diversify, the environments of the human races, irrespective of the geographical differences, since man has gradually learned to create his own environment wherever he lives. To become adapted to a colder climate, a race of animals grows warmer fur, and becomes genetically different from races which live in warmer climates. Man meets the same situation by building bigger fires and designing warmer clothes.

The steadily advancing improvements of communication and transportation have led to the increasing diffusion of genes across geographic race boundaries. Man is a migratory animal. His wandering propensities resulted in a biologically anomalous situation. In modern times several races, which formerly were separated in different countries, may now share the same territory. The situation is biologically anomalous because, in sexual organisms, races intercross when they find themselves living side by side, and this interbreeding results in fusion of the once separate races into a single variable population. On the other hand, distinct species often share the same territory without mixing. This is because species do not normally interbreed. If human races live together in the same territory without immediate fusion it is usually because the exchange of genes between them is impeded not by biological or geographical forces but by cultural ones. Whether such coexistence can continue indefinitely without fusion is doubtful. Some intermixture of race probably occurs whenever races meet. Cultural isolation is never as effective as is biological reproductive isolation.

The Adaptive Nature of Human Races

Among animals and among plants, races of a species diverge and become genetically different because they live in different environments. Natural selection is acting to adapt each race to its particular environment. The differences between breeds and varieties of domesticated animals and plants are due to artificial selection, or to a combination of both natural and artificial selections. They are bred to be different because their uses are to be different. Natural selection makes races adapted to their natural environments; artificial selection makes them adapted to human needs or whims.

Physical differences between human races arose chiefly through natural selection. When the old naturalists and anthropologists called the Negro race "the child of the African sun" they meant that the characteristics of this race were induced directly by the exposure of many generations to the geographic conditions of Africa. Modern evolutionists use the same symbolic expression to mean that most of the characteristics of the Negro race were forged by natural selection in response to the adaptive requirements of African environments. To be sure, modern anthropology and biology are unable to specify just what are, or were, the adaptive advantages of all racial traits observable among men. Why, for example, is it better to have coarse straight hair in eastern Asia and frizzy hair in Africa? Why are some American Indian tribes eagle-nosed and their near relatives snub-nosed?

The difficulty may be, in part, that these racial traits may have been adaptive in the primitive environments under which the race differentiation took place in times long past, rather than being adaptive in present environments. A simpler and more important explanation of the difficulty has been that, until recently, most anthropologists and biologists failed to realize that most of the racial traits in man are adaptive, and consequently they did not direct their investigations towards finding the adaptive functions of these traits. This remains largely true even now, but in a recent book Coon, Garn, and Birdsell have produced at least some hypothetical suggestions which may serve as working hypotheses in future studies.

Racial Differences in Psychic Traits

Few problems have been subject to dispute so long and so inconclusively as that of the existence of genetically conditioned differences in psychic traits between human races. Scientifically reliable data are far less abundant than are dogmatic pronouncements bearing on this issue.

An opinion shared by many (though not all) biologists and anthropologists is that although average differences in psychic traits between human populations may exist, such average differences are small compared to the individual differences between members of the same population. Just as most races contain people who are skinny, slim, corpulent, fat, and obese, so they contain people with various special abilities and people with no special ability, and people with high, average, and low general intelligence. The same is probably true for traits other than intelligence. It may be that some groups of people are, on the average, more inclined to be high-strung, while others are more placid; it may be that some special abilities, such as musical aptitude, are more widespread in some tribes than in others. But, again, more and less excitable people occur everywhere, even though in some cultures impulsive behavior is considered improper, while in others it is condoned and even encouraged. Musically sensitive and tone-deaf persons can probably be met with everywhere. The variability is induced by natural selection because every human society has many different functions that need to be performed; the interpersonal variability probably has both a genetic and a cultural basis.

All races of the human species share the fundamental human ability to acquire and to maintain culture. Ever since the human phase of evolution was reached, man's adaptation to his environments has occurred not so much by the modification of his body structures as by the exercise of his ingenuity. This is true even on the most primitive cultural levels known, and even more true in advanced civilizations. Man adapts himself to his environments, or adapts his environments to himself, chiefly by making use of his skills, inventions, knowledge, and understanding. This is certainly true of all races, and has been true since the start of cultural evolution. In evolutionary terms, this means that the pressure of natural selection has always been exerted towards the maintenance and improvement of those genotypes which confer on their possessors the capacity to acquire, to use, and to transmit culture. This fundamental educability is not a distinguishing mark of any one race; it is a common property of the human species.

To put it in another way, compared to races of animals, particularly domestic animals, the relative weight or importance of genetic differences between humans is reduced by the genetically controlled plasticity of human intellectual and emotional development. Does this argument amount to a denial of the existence of genetic variables in the formation of personality differences between individuals and groups? It certainly does not. The relative importance of heredity and environment in the development of individuals and populations is not a constant. It varies from trait to trait, from population to population, and from environment to environment. In uniform environments the importance of genetic differences becomes exaggerated, while with uniform genotypes, the environmental differences become the sole source of observable variability.

Applied to the development of human personality, this

means that under conditions of ideal equality of opportunity in education and living, the observed variance in personality traits would reflect the genotypic variability of the human beings concerned. The more the actual conditions deviate from the ideal of equality, the greater becomes the variation contributed by the factor of environmental inequality. Because of the remarkable plasticity of development patterns of the personality in man, the genotypic component of the variation becomes submerged in the environmentally conditioned variations. Equality of opportunity for all men is as yet a remote ideal. Hence, the differences between persons and groups in psychic traits may be ascribed to a large extent to environmental effects. The genetic differences would, however, loom larger and larger as equality was approached.

Common Denominators of Culture

Heredity and environment, and heredity and culture, are not mutually exclusive; they act jointly as determinants in the development of human personality and behavior. It has been pointed out that the biological heredity of the human species created the genetic basis which made cumulative learning, and hence culture, possible. This biological heredity conferred upon our species a high fitness, and was accordingly perpetuated and strengthened by natural selection.

It must now be emphasized that, although biological evolution has made cultural evolution possible, it has not determined what this cultural evolution should be. Cultural history is not biological history, in the sense that, given the genetic constitution which the human species actually has, human history could not have taken a variety of courses different from the course it actually took. The most important agents which propel human history are contained in that history itself, not in the stuff of which human genes are made. Historical events of the past could not be deduced, nor could future ones be predicted with any precision, only from a knowledge of the human genotype, no matter how complete.

The extent to which genetic differences between peoples have contributed to the emergence of differences between their cultures is another problem. This problem has not been solved, and it cannot be solved by dogmatic pronouncements. Such pronouncements have been numerous, while careful and unprejudiced studies have been conspicuously few. This is a matter for the future. For the time being, there is no convincing evidence that even the common denominators of all cultures are directly conditioned biologically. Professor Murdock has given the following list of these "common denominators," alphabetically arranged: "age-grading, athletic sports, bodily adornment, calendar, cleanliness training, community organization, cooking, cooperative labor, cosmology, courtship, dancing, decorative art, divination, division of labor, dream interpretation, education, eschatology, ethics, ethnobotany, etiquette, faith healing, family, feasting, fire making, folklore, food taboos, funeral rites, games, gestures, gift giving, government, greetings, hair styles, hospitality, housing, hygiene, incest taboos, inheritance rules, joking, kin-groups, kinship nomenclature, language, law, luck superstitions, magic, marriage, mealtimes, medicine, modesty concerning natural functions, mourning, music, mythology, numerals, obstetrics, penal sanctions, personal names, population policy, postnatal care, pregnancy usages, property rights, propitiation of supernatural beings, puberty customs, religious ritual, residence rules, sexual restrictions, soul concepts, status differentiation, surgery, tool making, trade, visiting, weaning, and weather control."

Some rather naive attempts have been made, chiefly by nineteenth-century biologists, to find a biological basis for some of these common denominators of cultures. The results were unconvincing, and modern anthropologists, as well as biologists, are justifiably skeptical about their usefulness. Indeed, should we look for genes which determine dancing, or magic, or puberty customs? Attempts have also been made to account for the universality of certain components of cultures by ascribing them to the instincts, or impulses, or drives, which occur in all representatives of the human species. There is no doubt that all humans are driven by hunger, sex, fear, vanity, and so on. But no satisfactory understanding of the origin of human intellectual capacities and of cultural patterns has yet been made from these premises. Many evolutionists, beginning with A. R. Wallace, the co-founder of Darwinism, felt constrained to admit the defeat of their attempts to understand the origin of man's intellect and culture on an evolutionary basis.

The difficulty may have been caused in part by an incorrect statement of the problem. It is futile to look for genes which caused mankind to invent bodily adornment, etiquette, incest taboos, numerals, or soul concept. Such genes do not exist, since, as we know, genes do not transmit "traits" or "characters." What they do transmit are developmental patterns, the realization of which is contingent upon the environment. Man has become the most successful of all biological species not because he acquired genes for cooking, for hygiene, for prenatal care, or for trade. His success has been due to genes which made him able to develop and to retain any of these and many other cultural traits; most of these traits proved useful, but some might have also been harmful, at least under some circumstances (e.g., dream interpretation or luck superstitions). The transition from the adaptive zone of a prehuman primate to the human adaptive zone was brought about by the development of the biological basis for the ability to use symbolic thought, language, to profit by experience, to learn, in short by the development of educability.

Human genes have accomplished what no other genes succeeded in doing. They formed the biological basis for a superorganic culture, which proved to be the most powerful method of adaptation to the environment ever developed by any species. In accepting Kroeber's designation of culture as "superorganic" no suggestion is made that culture is a product of a supernatural or an esoteric force (no such implications have been put in this expression by Kroeber either). All that this expression means is that the development of culture shows regularities *sui generis,* not found in biological nature, just as biological phenomena are subject to biological laws which are different from, without being contrary to, the laws of inorganic nature.

Evolutionary Humanism

It is unavoidable that the foregoing discussion will be regarded by some people as failing to come to grips with the really fundamental problem of man's uniqueness. We have occupied ourselves with matters as base and arid as genes and genotypes. But, do genes have any bearing at all on the higher values which make man's estate truly unique? Is there any biological basis, explanation, or justification for the ideas of right and wrong which only man possesses? No doubt the question is legitimate, and perhaps the greatest challenge which a biologist encounters has been stated as follows by Julian Huxley: "Medieval theology urged man to think of human life in the light of eternity—*sub specie aeternitatis.* I am attempting to re-think it *sub specie evolutionis.*" To which the present writer would like to add that evolution, too, will have to be thought about in the light of eternity, eternity in the light of evolution, and human life in the lights of both.

Some attempts in this direction have been made repeatedly since the time of Herbert Spencer. Darwin's theory came as a crowning achievement to the spectacular development of natural science in the nineteenth century. Following on the heels of the great discoveries in physics

...try, Darwin appeared, to some of his con-
...to have successfully done away with the
... (Darwin himself was under no such il-
...hat no problem seemed too difficult for
...ice. Spencer's *Principles of Ethics* stands
...ment to this surfeit of optimism. The decades
...ollowed ushered in some difficulties and also some
needed sophistication. The current of evolutionary naturalism, begun with Darwin and Spencer, became, however, an integral part of the scientific movement. The most
active modern exponent of evolutionary naturalism or of
evolutionary humanism, as he prefers to call it, is Julian
Huxley. To Huxley, Waddington, Chauncey Leake, and
several others, we owe modern versions of this viewpoint.
Huxley has even asserted that his evolutionary humanism
"is capable of becoming the germ of a new religion, not
necessarily supplanting existing religions but supplement-
ing them." This is probably claiming far too much. The
decision may well be left to the future.

The evolutionary approach has become an integral part
of the intellectual equipment of modern man because it
is indeed capable of yielding some ideas of broad philosophical interest and significance. About a century ago
Darwin proposed a theory of the evolutionary development of the biological species. Since then the idea of
evolution has become applied much more widely than in
the field of biology. On the one hand, the Cosmos itself is
now being thought about as a product of an evolutionary
development. On the other, it is not only man's bodily

frame but the whole Man that must be regarded as a result of an evolutionary process. Evolution is the method whereby Creation is accomplished.

Evolutionary Ethics

It has been said that "Man was formed for society." The seclusion of an anchorite is assuredly neither the usual nor the normal human environment. The environment of a member of our species is set by the society of which he is a member. He is influenced by his relations to other persons in the same society; in fact, interpersonal relations constitute the most important aspect of human environment. These relations often determine the ability of an individual to survive and to leave progeny. The interpersonal relations which prevail in a society or in a group within a society affect its chances for survival and perpetuation. These simple considerations have led many thinkers, from Darwin to our day, to suppose that man's behavior as a member of society is, like the structure and the physiology of his body, molded in the evolutionary process and controlled by natural selection. The basic assumption to this view has been stated most concisely by Leake as follows: "The probability of survival of a relationship between individual humans or groups of humans increases with the extent to which that relationship is mutually satisfying."

The greatest, although by no means the only, difficulty for this utilitarian explanation of ethics lies in understanding the nature and origin of the moral sense which every man, to some degree, has. Admiration of the good and disapprobation of the bad is ineradicable from the human mind. Regardless of whether a person does or does not live up to the standards of ethics accepted in his social environment, he usually feels that these standards have some validity which he cannot gainsay. Yet the kinds of behavior which many ethical codes hold most praiseworthy do not always promote the survival and welfare of the person who adopts them. Indeed, the selfish often prosper more than the generous, the cunning more than the truthful, and the cowards more than the brave. The rule that whatever promotes the survival and welfare of the individual is good, and whatever puts them in jeopardy is bad, is no safe guide in ethics. Yet such a rule would be expected to hold if ethics were a product of what nineteenth-century evolutionists called the survival of the fittest in the struggle for existence. There is a glaring conflict between the "gladiatorial theory of existence," seemingly implied in the evolutionary theory, and the Golden Rule, which, to most people, still stands as the most trenchant statement of the guiding principle of ethics. In 1893, T. H. Huxley admitted with admirable courage and sincerity that he was thwarted by the contradiction.

Ways towards a resolution of this apparent conflict were not opened up until it was realized that the "gladiatorial theory" is not only not a necessary part of the theory of natural selection, let alone a part of the theory of evolution, but is, in fact, invalid on purely biological grounds. Biological fitness is by no means always promoted by the ability to win in combat. It is much more likely to be furthered by the inclination to avoid combat, and in any case, it is measured in terms of reproductive success rather than in terms of the numbers of enemies destroyed. Moreover, not only individuals, but also groups of individuals, such as tribes and races, are units of natural selection. It is, then, at least conceivable that evolutionary processes may promote the formation of codes of ethics which, under some conditions, may operate against the interests of a few individuals but which favor the group to which these individuals belong. Biological analogies are readily available. Among ants, termites, and other social insects, an individual often sacrifices his life for the sake of the colony. In social insects most individuals do not reproduce, and natural selection favors the forms of behavior which increase the chances of survival of the colony, and particularly of its sexual members.

This, certainly, does not dispose of all the difficulties in understanding ethics on an evolutionary basis. In man, codes of morality and ethics vary from group to group. In a given group they may undergo changes with time, as history abundantly shows. Are we to conclude that, in man, natural selection favors the ethical codes which benefit the group at the expense of the individual? Such a view would leave unresolved the ethical paradox of conflicting interests between the individual and the society to which he belongs. We saw that the behavior of an ant is largely determined by its biological heredity, and that the ant has no choice but to act as it does. On the other hand, man is free to choose between various courses of action, and feels himself responsible for the choices he makes. He can choose to work for or against the society. Should he always sacrifice himself to the interest of his group, and does the group always have the right to expect its members to do so? This is, of course, one of the greatest problems facing mankind. All the great literatures and philosophies have struggled to resolve this conflict, and most of them have found that the only solution is to accept a divine sanction as the foundation of ethics. The crumbling of this foundation in our day leaves a terrible void in the human soul.

Julian Huxley has made a valiant attempt to find a substitute for divine sanction as the foundation of ethics. He proposes an evolutionary sanction instead. According to him, "The function of social ethics is, in biological terminology, phylogenetic, helping society to persist, to reproduce itself, and in some cases to change and to advance." The basis of "scientific" ethics is, then, the degree of agreement between the consequences of a given action and the evolutionary trend of the development of the human species. The rule becomes: "Anything which permits or promotes open development is right; anything which restricts or frustrates development is wrong. It is a morality of evolutionary direction," and: "In this light the highest and most sacred duty of man is seen as the proper utilization of the untapped resources of human beings."

Is Evolution Always Right?

No theory of evolutionary ethics can be acceptable unless it gives a satisfactory explanation of just why the promotion of evolutionary development must be regarded as the *summum bonum*. Indeed, any morality of evolutionary direction rests of necessity on our ability to determine what this direction has been and what it is at present. There is no single trend in evolution, but rather many different trends in different organisms. To be sure, some trends predominate in the evolution of some groups. Thus, the development of the cerebral functions, of intelligence, seems to have been the dominant trend in human evolution. Continuation of intellectual development becomes, then, a moral duty of mankind. But this is surely not the whole story. Human evolution has also involved many other trends, some of which were more constant than others, some which reversed themselves, and some which are of a degenerative character. Thus, there was for some time in the history of mankind a trend towards the differentiation of the human species into races, and towards biological divergence of these races. More recently, this trend was reversed because of the increasing mobility of human populations and of intermarriage between them, and human races began to converge. Which of these two trends should, then, be the basis of our ethics? And how about the allegedly great fertility of the intellectually less well-endowed persons and groups within human populations? If such a trend actually exists, surely it is more reasonable to think of combating it rather than assisting it.

Suppose, however, that future studies of human biology and evolution tell us exactly what the direction of evolution in general, and of human evolution in particular, has been. Just why should we take for granted that this direction, which we have not chosen, is good? The very fact that man knows that he has evolved and is evolving means that he is able to contemplate speeding up his evolution, slowing it down, stopping it altogether, or changing its direction. And his increasing knowledge and understanding of evolution may enable him to translate his thoughts into reality. Despite any exhortations to the contrary, man will not permanently deny himself the right to question the wisdom of anything, including the wisdom of his evolutionary direction. He may rebel against this direction, even though it may be shown to be a beneficial one. Just such an "unreasonable" rebellion was envisaged by Dostoevsky in his *Letters from the Underworld*. Man is likely to prefer to be free rather than to be reasonable. As Simpson put it: "There is no ethics but human ethics, and a search that ignores the necessity that ethics be human, relative to man, is bound to fail."

Determinism and Educability

As we have shown, there is ample evidence that the behavior of an individual animal towards other individuals of the same or of different species is in part genetically conditioned. Conspecific individuals have to co-operate with each other, at least at certain times, such as during periods of reproduction. Cooperation is especially prominent in social organisms, because social cohesion demands a certain minimum of cooperation among members of a society. Since social organization may increase the biological fitness of the species, natural selection may be expected to promote cooperative behavior.

The problem is to what extent will the behavior be inborn, resulting from biological heredity, and to what extent will it be conditioned in every generation by learning from other members of the society. Different solutions of this problem have been achieved by different organisms. Social insects offer many examples of behavior which is to a large extent inborn, and only to a limited extent learned. Conversely, human behavior is in the main genetically unfixed; it shows a remarkably high degree of phenotypic plasticity. It is acquired in the process of socialization, of training received from other individuals. Its base is set by the genes, but the direction and extent of its development are, for the most part, culturally, rather than biologically, determined.

The uncertainties of the nature-nurture problem are due precisely to the intricate blending of the inborn or genetic, and the acquired or cultural stimuli of behavior. The tender, protective, self-denying, passionate devotion felt by parents for their children may well be genetically conditioned. So may be the fact that the devotion felt by children, at least by grown-up ones, for their parents is usually less ardent than that felt by the parents towards the children. This is in no way contradicted by the fact that expressions of parental and filial devotion vary greatly from culture to culture, and that within a culture some parents may, under some circumstances, display a deficiency of parental feelings.

The manifestation of inborn drives in man depends on the cultural setting, just as the manifestation of any genetic trait may, to a greater or lesser extent, depend on the environment in which development takes place. The anthropologist Coon maintains that human nature was shaped by natural selection chiefly during the long, formative stage of the history of our species when men obtained their sustenance by hunting wild animals. "Our biological make-up is the same as theirs [Paleolithic hunters] and our biological needs were determined by natural selection over hundreds of thousands of years." This may well be right, but the progeny of these hunters developed agriculture, settled on land, built cities, invented industries and innumerable machines and gadgets, and finally rose to a point when they hold their own future evolution in their own brains and hands.

Attempts to discover a biological basis of ethics suffer from mechanistic oversimplification. Human acts and aspirations may be morally right or morally wrong, regardless of whether they assist the evolutionary process to proceed in the direction in which it has been going, or whether they assist it in any direction at all. But the matter is more subtle than that. Dostoevsky makes his Ivan Karamazov spurn the promise of the universe's evolution towards perfection and eternal harmony if this evolution must be promoted by the torture of just one innocent child. Ethics are a part of the cultural heritage of mankind, and consequently belong to the new human evolution, rather than to the old biological evolution. Moral rightness and wrongness have meaning only in connection with persons who are free agents, and who are consequently able to choose between different ideas and between possible courses of action. Ethics presuppose freedom.

Ethics and Freedom

Ethics, as such, have no genetic basis and are not the product of biological evolution. Natural selection has not propagated genes for ethics, or genes for inventing Euclidean geometry, propounding evolutionary theories, composing musical symphonies, painting landscapes, making a million dollars on Wall Street, loving the soil, or becoming a military leader. Such genes simply do not exist. Genes do not transmit and do not determine specific components of our cultural heredity.

The ability to study geometry, let alone higher mathematics, had no selective value in the ancestors of our species, and it is not certain that such abilities are biologically advantageous even at present. However, the ability of abstract thinking, or of perceiving causal relationships between events, did confer tremendous adaptive advantages on the human species. This basic ability has enabled man gradually to achieve a mastery over his environments, to develop ways and means to alleviate hunger, poverty, and disease. And the same basic ability has made possible the birth and development of science, art, philosophy, and religion. If natural selection has not developed genes for philosophy, it has favored genetic endowments which enable their carriers to become, among other things, philosophers. Science, art, philosophy, and religion are products of the basic intellectual powers of the human species. But their development, let alone the development of particular forms of science, art, philosophy, and religion which actually came into existence, was not contained in the human genotype or predestined by it.

This does not mean, of course, that biological evolution has reached its end and has been replaced by cultural evolution. Man of the Old Stone Age already had the genetic equipment needed to develop a culture; this fact has led some anthropologists to conclude that no further genetic progress has taken place in human evolution since the dawn of mankind. Surely, such a conclusion is not necessitated by the facts, and is most improbable on biological grounds. Our remote ancestors were biologically successful precisely because they came to possess the genetic wherewithal to acquire and to transmit rudiments of culture. Because of this adaptive success, the genetic equipment which makes culture possible is being maintained and reinforced by continuous selection going on in most human populations most of the time. We have discussed briefly the fears that, in modern times, natural selection no longer favors high intelligence in some human societies. Whether these fears are justified or not, the very possibility of their existence shows that the genetic basis of culture is not something immutable or incapable of improvement or deterioration.

The relative autonomy of cultural evolution from biological evolution lies in a different plane. Biological evolution has produced the genetic basis which made the new, specifically human, phase of the evolutionary process possible. But this new evolution, which involves culture, occurs according to its own laws, which are not deducible from, although also not contrary to, biological laws. The ability of man to choose freely between ideas and acts is one of the fundamental characteristics of human evolution. Perhaps freedom is even the most important of all the specifically human attributes. Human freedom is wider than "necessity comprehended," which is the only kind of freedom recognized by Marxists. Man has freedom to defy necessity, at least in his imagination. Ethics emanate from freedom and are unthinkable without freedom.

Ethics are, consequently, a human responsibility. We cannot rely on genes or on natural selection to guarantee that man will always choose the right direction of his evolution. This has been beautifully stated by Simpson in the following paragraph:

"Man has risen, not fallen. He can choose to develop his capacities as the highest animal and to try to rise still farther, or he can choose otherwise. The choice is his responsibility, and his alone. There is no automatism that will carry him upward without choice or effort and there is no trend solely in the right direction. Evolution has no purpose; man must supply this for himself. The means to gaining right ends involve both organic evolution and human evolution, but human choice as to what *are* the right ends must be based on human evolution. It is futile to search for an absolute ethical criterion retroactively in what occurred before ethics themselves evolved. The best human ethical standard must be relative and particular to man and is to be sought rather in the new evolution, peculiar to man, than in the old, universal to all organisms. The old evolution was and is essentially amoral. The new evolution involves knowledge, including the knowledge of good and evil."

Bibliography

Allee, W. C. Cooperation Among Animals. New York, Schumann, 1951.

Andrewartha, H. C., and L. C. Birch. The Distribution and Abundance of Animals. Chicago, University of Chicago Press, 1954.

Benedict, Ruth. Patterns of Culture. New York, New American Library, 1934.

Boyd, W. C. Genetics and the Races of Man. Boston, Little, Brown, 1950.

Childe, G. What Happened in History. Revised ed. London, Penguin, 1954.

Coon, C. S. The Story of Man. New York, Knopf, 1954.

—— "Some Problems of Human Variability and Natural Selection in Climate and Culture," American Naturalist, 89 (1955), 257–79.

—— S. M. Garn, and J. B. Birdsell. Races. Springfield, Ill.; Thomas, 1950.

Darlington, C. D. Facts of Life. London, Allen & Unwin, 1953.

Darwin, Charles. The Descent of Man. 1871.

—— On the Origin of the Species by Means of Natural Selection. 1859.

Dobzhansky, Th. Evolution, Genetics, and Man. New York, John Wiley, 1955.

138 BIBLIOGRAPHY

Dobzhansky, Genetics and the Origin of Species. New York, Columbia University Press, 1951.

—— "Evolution as a Creative Process." *Proceedings of the Ninth International Congress on Genetics* (1954), pp. 435–49.

—— "Human Races in the Light of Genetics." *International Social Science Bulletin* (UNESCO), 3 (1951), 660–63.

Frisch, K. Von. Bees. Ithaca, Cornell University Press, 1950.

Haskins, C. P. Of Societies and Men. London, Allen & Unwin, 1951.

Herskovits, M. J. Man and His Works. New York, Knopf, 1948.

Howells, W. W. Back of History. New York, Doubleday, 1954.

Huxley, Julian. Evolution in Action. New York, Harper, 1953.

Huxley, Thomas H., and Julian Huxley. Touchstone for Ethics. New York, Harper, 1947.

Kluckhohn, C., and O. M. Mowrer. "Culture and Personality," *American Anthropologist*, 46 (1944), 1–29.

Köhler, Wolfgang. The Mentality of Apes. 3d ed. New York, International Library of Sociology and Social Reconstruction, 1948.

Kroeber, A. L. "Sign and Symbol in Bee Communities," *Proceedings of the National Academy of Sciences*, 38 (1952), 753–57.

Kropotkin, P. Mutual Aid. Boston, Extending Horizons, 1955.

Leake, C. D., and P. Romanel. Can We Agree? Austin, Texas; University of Texas Press, 1950.

Lorenz, K. King Solomon's Ring. New York, Crowell, 1952.

Lush, Jay Laurence. "Genetics and Animal Breeding" in Genetics in the Twentieth Century, L. C. Dunn, ed. New York, Macmillan, 1951.

Murdock, G. P. "The Common Denominators of Cultures," in The Science of Man and the World Crisis, by Ralph Linton. New York, Columbia University Press, 1945.

Simpson, G. G. The Meaning of Evolution. New Haven, Yale University Press, 1949.

Spencer, Herbert. The Principles of Sociology. 3d ed. New York, 1896.

Stern, C. Principles of Human Genetics. San Francisco, Freeman, 1949.

Waddington, C. H. Science and Ethics. London, Allen & Unwin, 1942.

Weidenreich, F. Apes, Giants and Men. Chicago, University of Chicago Press, 1946.

Yerkes, R. M. and A. W. Yerkes. "Social Behavior of Infrahuman Primates," in Handbook of Social Psychology. Worcester, Mass., 1935.